digital TRANSFORMATION

digital *TRANSFORMATION*

The Essentials of e-Business Leadership

Keyur Patel
Mary Pat McCarthy

McGraw-Hill

NEW YORK   SAN FRANCISCO   WASHINGTON, D.C.   AUCKLAND   BOGOTÁ
CARACAS   LISBON   LONDON   MADRID   MEXICO CITY   MILAN
MONTREAL   NEW DELHI   SAN JUAN   SINGAPORE
SYDNEY   TOKYO   TORONTO

McGraw-Hill

A Division of The McGraw·Hill Companies

3 4 5 6 7 8 9 0   DOC/DOC   0 9 8 7 6 5 4 3 2 1 0

ISBN 0-07-136408-0

Designed by Michael Mendelsohn at MM Design 2000, Inc.
Printed and bound by R. R. Donnelley & Sons Company.

McGraw-Hill books are available at special quantity discounts to use as premiums and
sales promotions, or for use in corporate training programs. For more information, please
write to the Director of Special Sales, McGraw-Hill, 2 Penn Plaza,
New York, NY 10121. Or contact your local bookstore.

 This book is printed on recycled, acid-free paper
containing a minimum of 50% recycled, de-inked fiber.

All information provided is of a general nature and is not intended to
address the circumstances of any particular individual or entity. Although
we endeavor to provide accurate and timely information, there can be no
guarantee that such information is accurate as of the date it is received or
that it will continue to be accurate in the future. No one should act upon
such information without appropriate professional advice after a thorough
examination of the facts of a particular situation.

Acknowledgements

This book could not have been written without the candid and insightful interviews granted us by Peter Boit, Vinton Cerf, John Chambers, Clayton Christensen, Amir Hartman, Vinod Khosla, Daniel Schulman, Roger Siboni, Charles Wang and David Wetherell. We are indebted to each of these gracious and talented e-business leaders. To Rob Brownstein, who contributed much to the writing of this document, we are extremely grateful. Our colleagues, Mark Carleton, Mark Goodburn, Joni Kahn, Rod McGeary, Tim Pearson, Ed Rodriguez and Terri Santisi provided valuable assistance at critical stages of the book's development. We thank Gino Lee, Brittany Walker, Kenneth Jamora, and Terence Lan for their creative artwork. Leslie Paladin and George Ledwith provided important marketing and public relations assistance. Our project manager, Marie Glenn, kept confusion in check while battling the many logistical challenges of producing this book. Thank you all.

— Keyur Patel
Mary Pat McCarthy
April, 2000

Contents

Foreword

We are in the midst of an Internet Revolution that will have an impact as big, if not bigger, than the Industrial Revolution. Today's revolution is leveling the playing field and creating unprecedented opportunities for countries, companies and individuals around the world. The result is an economy in which agility and the ability to adapt to change, not size, geographic location, or physical assets are the keys to success and survival.

In just five years since the introduction of the World Wide Web, the Internet economy already rivals the size of century-old sectors such as energy, automotive and telecommunications. Milestones that took up to 100 years to achieve in the Industrial Age are occurring at a staggering pace in this new economy.

It is increasingly evident that the adoption of Internet applications is the key to future growth. The countries and companies that will survive are those that learn to harness the power of the Internet to create a competitive advantage.

This book outlines why some companies have excelled in the Internet economy and why some companies have missed on execution. It also offers powerful insights into what it takes to be an Internet Economy leader.

Four years ago, Cisco predicted that the Internet would change the way we work, live, play and learn. Today, 85 percent of our orders — or over $40 million a day — are transacted over the Web. I truly believe that this book is a valuable resource for anyone looking to compete successfully in the new economy.

> — John Chambers
> President and CEO,
> Cisco Systems, Inc
> April, 2000

Introduction

You're reading this introduction, so we've got to presume you have an interest in e-business. To be sure, there is no shortage of books extolling the virtues of e-business and its technology underpinnings. This isn't one of them.

We won't talk about network equipment, software systems, or Web servers, because that isn't the kind of knowledge that will help you succeed. And we won't advise you to copy any particular dot.com's e-business strategy. That's the prescription for followship, not leadership.

We do write about e-business and why you should be taking it very seriously. And we will discuss the advantages and disadvantages of spinning off a separate e-business entity. We also want to say at the outset that this book is full of opinions — ours as well as those of several well-known business executives. This book is not meant to be an exhaustive, scholarly, precise analysis of all the nuances of e-business strategies and business models. That's because there were already a handful of new nuances the day after the book was published. But it's also because e-business is inherently imprecise. Besides, in the time it takes to be precise, someone else will have usurped your opportunity with a less-than-perfect solution.

Your commitment to e-business should either be profound or non-existent. There is no middle ground. Think about how many e-businesses you know of that sell books online. After Amazon.com and Barnes & Noble.com, who's left? Think about how many e-businesses you know of that provide online auctions. After eBay, how many more jump right to mind?

The Net is no place for also-rans. There is no opportunity to win if you're trying to be Amazon.com or eBay. But, like all the possible moves in a game of chess, the Net and the new economy it has spawned offer countless opportunities to do something different. And to quote a line in *Net Ready*, the recent book by Amir Hartman and John Sifonis, "Different isn't always better, but the best is always different." (Hartman is Managing Director of Internet Strategy at Cisco and Sifonis, directs Cisco's Internet Business Solutions Group.)

> **"Different isn't always better, but the best is always different."**
> — Amir Hartman & John Sifonis

Because of its penchant for lowering the cost of information dissemination and transactions, the Net is a petri dish for innovation in the creation of business value. Rather than focusing on current business rules and supporting technologies, we'll focus on things you can do to change the rules of the game. You can create entirely new value chains that have non-linear relationships. You can leverage brick-and-mortar legacies into click-and-order primacies. The Net offers many ways to separate form from function and to provide customers with unfettered function.

We'll look at what it takes to make a profound commitment to e-business. We're talking about digital transformation. If you think being "in e-business" means suturing on an e-commerce appendage to your body corporate, then think again. We promise you that won't work. You've got to become "an e-business." You've got to be prepared to let that e-business commitment ripple through and shake up that body corporate. And like experiencing an 8.0 earthquake, you must be prepared for the rearrangement that will inevitably occur.

If you currently run a brick-and-mortar business, be assured that a profound commitment to e-business will have a profound effect upon your existing business practices. If it doesn't, there's something wrong. Being an e-business is not about changing the way you do one thing, or simply adding a new channel to your existing channels. It is about changing everything. It is often a bet-the-company gambit. Charles Schwab won because it was willing to risk cannibalizing its old ways of doing business, while its competitors were not. Cisco Systems won because, from its CEO on down, e-business became a crusade that transformed the entire company.

Like any credible business book, this one has its case histories. But, here, the intent is not to have you copy a strategy that worked for any particular company. Rather, the intent is to help you see the common success factors that underscored each company's efforts. One of the success factors is vision. Another is leadership. Many e-business efforts have failed because of the ad hoc nature of their strategy and management. They were like trucks careening down a highway with no drivers, no road maps and no real destinations in mind.

The nature of the Net is destined to change. Its demographics are changing. Its technology underpinnings are changing. Its infrastructure is changing. While the foundation of the World Wide Web was laid with Tim Berners-Lee's creation of HTML, the hypertext markup language that enables point-and-click navigation online, it was Netscape co-founder Marc Andreessen's development of the Mosaic browser, along with Eric Bina's programming savviness, that set the spark for today's Internet explosion.

Being an e-business is not about changing the way you do one thing, nor simply adding a new channel to your existing channels. It is about changing everything.

Who will be the next Andreessen? What will be the next Mosaic? How will the Net evolve? What effect will XML and wireless access have upon e-business? How do you prepare for the unpredictable? Even big players find themselves unprepared sometimes. Just ask Microsoft's Bill Gates and AOL's Steve Case. Neither anticipated the speed or extent of the Internet's effect upon their markets. Even with some knowledge about the near-term future, there is no guarantee of smooth sailing. But it may help you avoid being blindsided, and it may ignite some visions about new value creation, improved efficiencies and enhanced customer interaction.

When you finish this book, you'll know what it takes to win at e-business — and the rewards are compelling. But there are two prerequisites: courage and innovation. These traits are critical if you are to accept the inevitable cannibalization of parts of your current business and their replacement by more efficient, highly valued aspects.

But take heart. As marketing luminary Peter Drucker said, "It is both cheaper and more profitable to obsolete yourself than it is to let your competitor do it for you." And, like the phoenix, the e-business that rises from the ashes will be a much stronger contender in the new economy of the 21st Century.

So, let's move forward. You've seen them all. Companies whose stock opened at $6 per share and, within a year or two, is selling at close to $300 per share. Thirty-something CEOs joining the mega-millionaire club seemingly overnight.

And you've seen the statistics. More than 200 million Net users, with millions more going online every month. The Internet has reached 50 million users in far less time than did television, radio or personal computers.

You've seen AOL initiate a merger with Time-Warner. You've read that the number of people making online purchases has increased significantly over the last year. You've seen Yahoo! announce record profits in its last calendar quarter of 1999. And Amazon's "brand" recognition is a Web legend, even though profits still elude the company and it has lost nearly $600 million since it started.

Wall Street has had a seemingly insatiable hunger for dot.com stocks. And practically every CEO in the Fortune 1000 is putting e-business near the top of their priority lists.

Something is definitely going on out there. And no one wants to be the last one on the block to embrace it. But hold on. Before you either plunge headfirst into the maelstrom or order a complete makeover of your current e-business strategy, take a deep breath and continue reading. As you already know, there is a big difference between an emotional decision and an informed one. This book is all about making informed e-business decisions.

There are those who say the Internet is a magical place that is transforming practically everything about our lives — how we learn, how we have fun, how we shop, how we think. There are others who say the Web is just another channel to use, and we shouldn't blow it out of proportion. We think they are both correct. In fact, every perception of the Web is correct, because, like the elephant being groped by blindfolded people, it feels different from every side and angle.

The Web has different implications for companies that plan to engage in business-to-consumer (b2c) marketing and sales than it does for those who use it for business-to-business (b2b) purposes. Yet they all share the Web's penchant for keeping communication and transaction costs low. The difference is in those purposes behind the communications and transactions.

The most "wrong headed" notion is the one that says, "Build it and they will come." Even Amazon.com, with arguably the Web's highest name recognition, is spending several million dollars through traditional advertising to bolster its customer base. Did you see how many dot.coms were advertising at millions of dollars a pop for a 30-second TV spot on Super Bowl XXXIV?

A Web presence is absolutely no guarantee of increased sales or expanded markets. For example, both IBM and Levi Strauss have stopped using the Web for online sales of PCs and clothing, respectively. Ask yourself why. We asked Roger Siboni, CEO of E.piphany. He thinks it was mostly an issue of channel conflict for IBM, but he shook his head about Levi's, saying, "I'm mystified by Levi's announcement, because the Web is such a natural distribution channel for them."

There's another misplaced idea that brick-and-mortar companies are at a natural disadvantage compared with born-on-the-Web companies. But you simply cannot generalize. Certainly, Barnes & Noble has a different cost structure than Amazon.com, but Barnes & Noble can offer its customers the convenience of returning books purchased online to any of its retail stores, whereas Amazon.com cannot.

Selling groceries online is another area where an existing infrastructure may be far more important than any Web-only strategy. For example, a born-on-the-Web grocery business will have to create alliances with neighborhood markets, much as Priceline.com has done in New York City and Philadelphia.

But an established national grocery chain already has that infrastructure and can concentrate on e-business strategy and tactics, rather than building infrastructure.

...the average new online user visits 100 Web sites, bookmarks 14 and stops bothering to search after that. How do you ensure that your Web site is one of the 100 visited, much less one of the 14 bookmarked?

Similarly, Cheap Tickets must issue printed airline tickets that are delivered by Airborne Express. As a result, they do not book reservations for departures less than five days ahead. American Airlines, on the other hand, offers its AA.com customers electronic tickets. Therefore, they can conceivably handle online orders within hours of a flight, rather than days.

Of course, not every physical-space concept will play on the Web. For example, one of the attractions of shopping malls is the aggregation of diverse retailers within the same enclosed area. There is certainly a convenience factor in being able to drive to one location and find one parking space. Web shopping malls, on the other hand, offer only the convenience of an aggregation of URL links. The customer doesn't have to leave his or her browser to go to any other retail URL. So, the added convenience factor these URL aggregators provide is minimal, at best.

You've read about the millions of new users who go online each month and the thousands of new Web sites that join them. One popular notion is that Internet users are somehow much better informed than their pedestrian counterparts. To be sure, there are Web sites that provide side-by-side comparisons of life insurance policies, automobiles, appliances, mortgages and the like. Do you know which ones? Does the person new to the Web know which ones?

Just go to three search-engine sites — Yahoo!, Alta Vista and Excite, for example — and enter the same key words. Then compare the first 20 links each of them returns. Great correlation, right? Wrong. And, as the Web is flooded with more and more URLs and pages, the search disparity grows.

"Okay," you say. "In time, users will find what they're looking for." Then you see the statistics that show that the average new online user visits 100 Web sites, bookmarks 14 and stops bothering to search after that. How do you ensure that your Web site is one of the 100 visited, much less one of the 14 bookmarked? The obstacles are immense and growing bigger every minute.

One of the problems with trying to organize the Web is its freeform underpinnings. In contrast, the telephone company knew exactly who was connected to its wires and could print very precise — and comprehensive — directories. About the only control that exists on the Internet is the allocation of domain names. Every attempt by a company in the US to exert some control over access to the Internet has at least raised the eyebrows of people at federal regulatory agencies.

The very privacy that Internet users hold on to with the tenacity of a dog and its bone is also a major impediment to any attempt to organize the Net. For b2c companies, the challenge is to get permission from privacy-conscious users to market to them, and, before that, to figure out how to get them to your site.

Now, most of the problems alluded to, thus far, are really problems for b2c e-businesses. And none of them need be showstoppers. We mention them simply to press the point that b2c e-business is neither simple nor foolproof. It takes more than a jazzy Web site to excel at e-tailing. It also takes a thorough understanding of the current state of e-tailing affairs and the identification of new ways to interact with customers — ways that those customers value. It will also take a thorough understanding of your current business model (assuming you have one) and identification of ways to inject greater efficiency into your business, even if it means turning your business model on its head (and it probably will).

As we mentioned earlier, b2b e-businesses have different Web priorities. Their concern is less about driving consumers to their Web sites and more about using the Web to shorten the order-to-delivery cycle, to reduce their cost of sales, to reduce their overall operating costs and to increase their overall profitability.

In many cases their communities of interest (COINs) are well-established. Agilent, Hewlett-Packard's spin-off of its non-computer-related business units, mirrors the pre-computer HP. Test-and-measurement instruments are a major product area, and engineers are part of its COIN. The typical engineer looking for information about a logic analyzer knows enough to enter www.agilent.com in a Web browser. These engineers would also know about www.tektronix.com. Neither Agilent nor Tektronix needs to spend millions of dollars on TV advertising to drive their prospective buyers to their sites. Similarly, neither Intel nor AMD needs to advertise its site to prospective microprocessor purchasers.

These and other b2b businesses have other priorities than keywords and search engines. When they built Web sites, their prospective customers did come. For these companies and others in the b2b space, the Web is far more than another commercial channel. It is an opportunity for them to experiment with new business models, to reconstruct their supply chains for lower-latency responsiveness, to attack front-office costs, to be different.

Remember, the b2b world already has experience with electronic business. It was trying to make a go of electronic data interchange (EDI) long before the advent of the Web. The obstacles, however, were platform dependencies and industry-specific standards. The Internet has effectively eliminated both of these obstacles. Now you can quickly create a networked supply chain without worrying about whether desktop units are PCs or Unix workstations, nor whether servers are Unix-based or Windows NT-based.

As you'll see, whether your interests are b2c or b2b, some e-business principles are universally applicable; others are b2c- or b2b-specific. Regardless of the nature of your business, if it existed before the World Wide Web, then a commitment to e-business will require fundamental rather than cosmetic change.

Statistics also show that when a visitor leaves a Web site dissatisfied, that visitor never returns. So one universal principle is that it is better not to have a Web presence than to have a mediocre Web presence.

A Kmart located 50 miles from the nearest Wal-Mart need not worry too much about differentiating itself from Wal-Mart. But every dot.com is equally convenient from your browser. Differentiation is not important — it's absolutely critical.

Statistics also show that when a visitor leaves a Web site dissatisfied, that visitor never returns. So one universal principle is that it is better not to have a Web presence than to have a mediocre Web presence. The first costs you nothing. The second costs you plenty. And neither produces incremental revenues.

Read on and see what being an e-business winner entails.

- ☐ What is "vision" in the context of e-business, and how do you get and apply it?
- ☐ What is digital transformation, and how does it change your business?
- ☐ What are the challenges for b2b companies and b2c companies in making a digital transformation?
- ☐ How do you prepare for the unpredictable?

CHAPTER 1

Who's Winning at e-Business?

Everyone wants to be a winner. But what exactly does that mean in the context of e-business? Is it about size, profits, or market share? Is it about name recognition, Web site "hits," or the percentage a stock price increases? It's all of these and more. So who is an e-business winner?

D epending on your criteria, you might have picked Amazon.com, Yahoo!, eBay or AOL. We bet most of you didn't pick Cisco or Intel, though. Your oversight might be due to lumping Cisco and Intel into the brick-and-mortar side of things. Or maybe you were unaware that Intel and Cisco are e-businesses. If so, you certainly have an excuse because the media seems to be drawn to the b2c (business-to-consumer) dot.coms (the born-on-the-Web companies), while largely ignoring the b2b (business-to-business) community. And why not? Routers and microchips are less entertaining than online bookstores, portals, auctions and whatever category AOL falls into this month.

$1 BILLION-PER-MONTH, ONLINE

Did you know that Cisco sells about 80 percent of its products online? Did you know that Cisco rakes in about a billion dollars a month from those sales? Those results put Cisco's e-business income at about two-and-one-half times the total revenues of all the 180 or so born-on-the-Web dot.coms put together. At the same time, Cisco has slashed its operating costs by putting virtually everything online. Plus, the king of Internet hardware has transformed its supply chain from the traditional linear model into a non-linear model. That is, the hierarchy of a traditional supply chain has been replaced by a model where communication among all the participants is not only possible, but encouraged. (See figure 1.) The upshot is a significant reduction in order-to-delivery cycle times — about 75 percent, according to Cisco's president and CEO, John Chambers.

Everyone has heard of "Intel inside," but few outside of Intel's COIN (communities of interest) have an inkling about the success of www.intel.com. Intel developed its b2b Web-based capabilities in early 1998, and within three months of the Web site launch, it was selling more than $1 billion worth

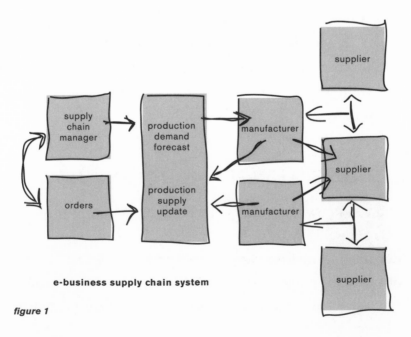

e-business supply chain system

figure 1

of product per month. The Web site caters to small- to medium-sized original equipment manufacturers, known as OEMs, and Intel's distributors. These sales intermediaries are able to check prices, view product road maps and buy products through a password-protected, customized Web site. The most immediate benefits are reductions in the transaction costs of products sold, and fewer errors in order processing and the order-to-delivery cycle.

We chose to briefly describe Cisco's and Intel's e-business prowess primarily because we knew that, for some of you, this is new information. In the words of Rodney Dangerfield, b2b e-businesses "don't get no respect" — at least not from the media. Yet it is the b2b sector that is really pushing the Web to new levels of diversity and reaping many of the benefits that today's Web makes possible. "Three years ago, people thought it would be business-to-consumer companies leading e-commerce on the Web," says Cisco's CEO John Chambers, "but it wasn't." Chambers sees a two- to three-year period before b2c catches up with where b2b is now. And CMGI's CEO, David Wetherell, believes the b2b sector will always dominate in e-business revenues and transactions "just as they do in the non-Web world."

ACHIEVING COMPETITIVE ADVANTAGE IN OVERNIGHT DELIVERY

Another e-business winner is Federal Express. With the competition growing among FedEx, Airborne, DHL and the US Postal Service, each was trying to differentiate its services.

FedEx was first to create a private wireless network that tied all of its operations together, from package reception, to routing, to delivery. And FedEx was first to create a Web-based, interactive interface that lets customers track their own shipments instantly. It was simply a matter of time before FedEx integrated its Web-based and private network applications so that customers could print out their own airbills without having to talk to anyone. Once the customer completes the airbill and clicks on a button, the appropriate driver is notified to make the pickup.

But FedEx has taken its e-business even further by allying itself with numerous companies to provide warehousing, picking, packing and delivery as a fully integrated part of the supply chain. So, in addition to using the Web to make its operations more efficient, FedEx is using its e-business infrastructure to push its services further up the food chain.

ALTERING THE PLAYING FIELD IN ELECTRONICS DISTRIBUTION

Another e-business winner is Ingram Micro, an electronics distribution e-business. Ingram Micro uses the Web to supply its technology resellers in the US, Europe, Latin America and Asia. It fields 78 distribution centers in strategic locations that, in aggregate, fulfill 150,000 shipments per day, leading the distribution industry in fill rate and same-day shipping capabilities.

One of Ingram Micro's value creation services is what it calls "pre-order management," which makes it possible for resellers to generate end-user quotes and send them, electronically, to their customers. This is yet another example of removing some of the latency from the supply chain.

Ingram Micro attempts to provide value at every step in the supply chain by offering virtual warehousing and logistics to smooth the way for manufacturers and resellers to more profitably assemble, store and ship their products. Like FedEx, Ingram Micro moves further up the food chain by offering inventory management, system configuration and financial services that enable its reseller partners to take advantage of new opportunities quickly. By providing its customers with outsourced business-critical functions, Ingram Micro helps their customers save money and spend their profits on their core operations. In other words, Ingram Micro is looking at their business from a completely new point-of-view, rewriting the rules and changing the nature of global distribution.

This is what e-business winners do. They:

☐ take a holistic view of their businesses and

☐ a realistic view of the Internet, then

☐ find ways to innovate and

☐ create new value for their customers.

For Cisco and Intel, the pace of new product development is unrelenting. Their e-business strategies enable them to keep pace with their markets' abilities to absorb new products. E-business allows them to provide more highly valued customer service. It gives them a more customer-centric view of future product requirements. And it lets them lower their operating costs. The results are:

- ☐ more loyal customers

- ☐ higher revenues, rising profits and

- ☐ increased shareholder value.

On the other hand, FedEx and Ingram Micro are using e-business to:

- ☐ differentiate their services from competitors and

- ☐ increase their competitive advantages.

By offering to take on more of their customers' front-office and back-office functions, they create loyalties that grow deeper and are more immutable. They also raise the table stakes for their competitors who want to stay in the game.

We could describe other e-business winners, but the point is that all of these winners have certain broad things in common. They did not approach e-business with an ad hoc attitude. They carefully considered what they wanted to accomplish, then drilled down to specifics to create the projects that would culminate in an e-business.

Although these companies take their e-business transformations very seriously, they didn't get caught up in analysis paralysis. They understood that e-business is not about stasis. It's not about precedence. It's not about entropy. At Cisco, for example, any e-business project that cannot be done by five people within 90 days is unacceptable. This is what they call "ruthless execution." If a project fails the ruthless execution test, it may be dropped, or it may be broken up into sub-projects that can pass the test. Regardless, no one at Cisco expects immediate perfection. They understand that time-to-market, even with less than perfect implementation of a plan, is far better than perfection banging at a closed window of opportunity.

The foregoing is not to say that Yahoo!, Amazon.com, AOL and eBay are not winners. They are. By being first with innovations in their markets, creating new categories and adding value to their products and services, they have, according to Cisco's Amir Hartman and John Sifonis, authors of *Net Ready*, gained the benefits of:

□ higher levels of investment

□ investors of a higher stature

□ alliances with partners of a higher stature and

□ the best choices among prospective employees.

If we measured these four companies with the same yard-stick as Cisco and Intel, despite their impressive month-to-month increases in new customers and revenues, we would find that they have yet to finesse their process models to yield truly impressive profit levels. After all, just about any company can increase its market share significantly by losing substantial amounts of money on each sale. The question is, for how long?

So, when we talk about excelling at e-business, we mean more than just achieving brand- or channel-equity alone. We mean achieving greater efficiencies, higher profits, better customer relationships and increased value. It doesn't matter whether you are a b2c or a b2b company. Ultimately, your e-business excellence will depend upon proficiency in all business areas, not just one or two.

e-Business Excellence Yields:

☐ Greater efficiencies

☐ Higher profits

☐ Better customer relationships

☐ Increased value

....

CHAPTER 2

The Vision Thing

Your e-business won't just happen. You've got to have a vision of what you hope to accomplish. That vision should be much like the image of a house that you want designed, as it appears in your mind's eye before you start working with an architect. From that vision, you can reverse engineer the functions you'll need to make it happen. Forget about right brain and left brain. No one has a better idea of what's happening in your industry than you do. No one can identify an opportunity to create new value better than you can. And it all starts with a vision.

About 14 years ago, Apple Computer produced a video-tape about the future of computing. There was only one scene: a college professor's office in the year 2011. In it, the professor had a device shaped like a paper notebook that answered his phone, took messages, and communicated with him through a voice-recognition and voice-synthesis "agent."

In the span of a few minutes, the professor was able to prepare a presentation correlating the shrinking of Brazil's Amazon rain forest with an increase in air pollution worldwide. He was also able to share this dynamically edited presentation with a colleague hundreds of miles away, in real time. The information for the presentation was gathered in seconds by searching through a combination of university libraries, and it appeared that he had done all of this wirelessly.

> You've got to have a vision of what you hope to accomplish.

Thus, in 1986, nearly a decade before the Web's "Big Bang," Apple envisioned a world of people connecting, sharing information and using a spoken natural-language interface. Yet, at the time, most computer users had huge desktop machines running command-line (MS DOS) software. Interestingly, though, virtually every one of the technologies featured in that video — voice synthesis, voice recognition, internetworking, active-matrix displays, wireless data networking — had in fact reached technology status and were no longer still within basic research boundaries. Apple's visionaries simply combined them in a way that made sense, after extrapolating where those technologies might be by 2011.

We mention Apple's video because, once again, vision is a key success factor in excelling at e-business. It has been said that "It's not the destination, it's the journey," but for e-business, it's both. You've got to envision what you want to achieve before setting hammer to nail.

It can start with an idea such as buy.com's, claiming to sell products at "the lowest prices on earth." Or it can be a reverse auction idea like Priceline.com's, where buyers state what they are willing to spend for an airline ticket or a few nights at a hotel, then Priceline.com finds an airline or hotel willing to accept that price. An online auction is eBay's vision, while matching automobiles to buyers is the idea behind autobytel.com.

The idea cannot stop there. What does buy.com have to do to ensure it always sells at the lowest prices on earth? What kinds of alliances must it forge? What categories of products should it sell? Does buy.com simply act as a broker, transparently sending order information on to its various vendors, or does it actually acquire, warehouse and ship from its own facilities? These are the kinds of questions that emerge as you look beyond an overarching vision.

SIMILAR VISIONS, DIFFERENT BUSINESS MODELS

It's not unusual for two companies to have similar visions, but it is unlikely that these visions will lead to similar solutions. Take Sears.com and brandwise.com, for example.

In the consumer marketplace, brandwise.com decided to create a business that matches appliances with customers' requirements. Their Web site lets you select appliance categories, search by pre-defined characteristics (such as gas or electric cooktops), then compare prices, sizes and appearances. But the user doesn't purchase from brandwise.com. Instead, brandwise.com merely directs the user to appliance dealers in their vicinities that carry the particular brand and model they have chosen. Guess who pays for the referral?

Sears has a Web site that lets users do the same thing as brandwise.com. Users can select a category, limit the search by characteristics and compare features of selected brands and models. Sears's own brand is always among the choices and users can purchase the appliance online.

Two very similar visions, two distinctly different business models. One is an information aggregator and referrer; the other is an information aggregator and e-tailer. In terms of implementing their e-businesses according to their visions, brandwise.com and Sears.com both succeeded. But anyone who suggests that their playing field is level is mistaken. Sears has significant brand equity, and it offers more than just its own line of Kenmore appliances, from which it likely earns a profit too. Brandwise.com has more of an impartial feel because it doesn't sell anything, however it also does not provide the order and fulfillment steps.

VISIONING

Can you imagine developing a product with no clear idea of its size, shape and function set? Or, can you imagine creating a service without defining its content and scope? Well, you cannot hope to establish a winning e-business without a clear, succinct, statement of vision. To be sure, arriving at that vision is anything but an exact science, and one company's method may not work for another. However, this is a critical first step. Toward that end, visioning can be done in-house or as part of a consulting engagement. We'll take a look at both.

IMAGINEERING – AN IN-HOUSE VISION GENERATOR

In the UK, Orange might best be described as a mobile telephone company. But Orange has adopted "imagineering" as its way to identify and describe its "destination." According to an influential "imagineer" and member of its executive team, "We try to avoid thinking about how to project our current business in our current market. If we myopically think of Orange as a mobile phone company, that's just what it will stay. Instead, we think of what we do well and what our customers would like us to be for them. Ultimately, we aim to be their lifestyle partner. We are customer-led — always walking in our customers' shoes. But sometimes (here comes the heresy), we have to take the lead, simply because today's customer does not know what she or he will want tomorrow, and it will be our responsibility to lead them there. Finally, we try to escape the tyranny of product development and, instead, think in terms of services and solutions."

A little more than two years ago, Orange created its Imaginarium, the members of which were charged with seeing their business in new and different ways. The members are called "ambassadors," and what qualifies them for membership is "the way their minds work." At Orange, "We recruit from Manchester to Mars."

A KPMG VISION METHODOLOGY

At KPMG, we too have developed and refined a process that has been very successful at e-vision generation. Before we describe it, though, we need to put it in the context of a complete e-business effort. Our approach to e-business strategy is an all-encompassing one, designed to develop an integrated enterprise from vendors and suppliers to customers, and focused around the b2b and b2c aspects of an organization.

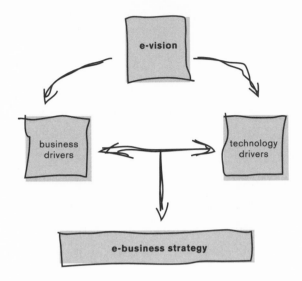

figure 2

As part of the process, we define and prioritize the business requirements, which allows us to validate and align the technical foundations of the company's current infrastructure.

We then develop a clear migration strategy and brand messaging with the goal of compelling the appropriate constituencies to take advantage of the e-business's infrastructure on the Web. The process flow begins with the e-vision, leading to the identification of the business and technology drivers, then culminating in the formulation of the e-business strategy. (See figure 2.)

The e-vision is derived from careful consideration of customer feedback, benchmark data, usage statistics, competitive analysis, customer needs, market forces and current capabilities. (See figure 3.)

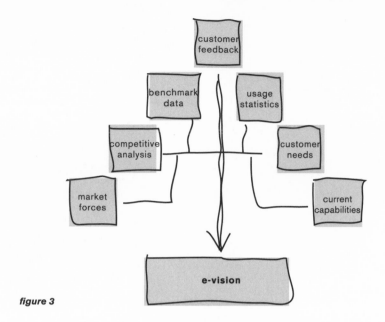

figure 3

Our objective is not necessarily for you to adopt our approach, but to recognize that the process is neither cavalier nor exhaustive.

PUTTING VISION TO USE

Using a similar approach, for example, FedEx may have found that enough of its customers were glad to hand off some of their back-office functions. The competitive analysis would have revealed that its competitors were not already doing that.

They may also have learned that customers wanted the ability to track shipments directly. At the time, though, direct tracking may not have been a feature of FedEx's service. However, the "current capabilities" scrutiny would have shown that, by using the Web, FedEx could add direct tracking quickly and at relatively low cost.

These findings would have underscored an e-vision that said, "We will give our customers more direct control over their shipping, while also giving them ways to offload more of the pre-shipping and shipping tasks." If FedEx had already been leaning toward that vision, the process would have validated that plan. Remember, the goal here is not absolute correlation and perfection. It's about finding opportunities to create new value, about innovative ways to make it happen and about doing it before someone else does it first.

In our process, we follow the e-vision with analysis of the business drivers that are implied by the e-vision. Among these may be:

☐ personalization

☐ return-on-investment

☐ profiling

☐ segmentation

☐ experience modeling (offline/online behavior patterns) and

☐ expanded business opportunities.

Then we look at the technology drivers implied by the e-vision. These typically include:

☐ systems and networks

- ☐ Web architecture

- ☐ business infrastructure

- ☐ technology components and

- ☐ Web technology strategy.

The resulting e-business strategy is an interweaving of business drivers and technology drivers that can help make the vision real.

Once again, we cannot overstate the importance of an e-business vision. It is the starting point. From a clearly articulated vision it is much easier to move forward, synthesizing the business and technology drivers that will support it. That, in turn, creates a well-defined e-strategy upon which to build an e-business.

e-Business Creation Process

- ☐ Vision

- ☐ Synthesis of business and technology drivers

- ☐ Strategy

- ☐ Implementation

....

CHAPTER 3

Transformation

As we noted in the introduction, you must either make a profound commitment to e-business or you will be better served by doing nothing at all. A profound commitment means following your vision with resolve. This is not the time for conditional commitment. If you can't complete a digital transformation in one fell swoop, it's alright to do it in increments. Just recognize that there is no turning back, once you take each step.

DIGITAL
TRANSFORMATION

At KPMG, we've named the process by which a company becomes an e-business "digital transformation." By that we mean more than the name would imply. Certainly, e-business is inextricably tied to the Web and the distribution of information in digital formats. Therefore, at a fundamental level, digital transformation refers to the conversion of all information — text, images, audio and video — into digital formats that can be exchanged, stored, indexed and "data-based."

But digital transformation means more than that. Along with the digital conversion will be changes to business processes associated with them. For example, information formerly exchanged as text on paper, such as an order form, can now be exchanged as a digital file and distributed to several "subscribers" simultaneously, without first having to be copied.

THE FOUR "C"S OF DIGITAL TRANSFORMATION

On a business-wide basis, digital transformation will encompass the four "C"s:

☐ commerce

☐ content

☐ community

☐ collaboration

It will transform the way we transact (commerce), the information we use (content), the people we interact with (community) and the ways we interact with them (collaboration). (See figure 4.)

We've found that the successful e-business strategies all involve digital transformation measured against two axes: value and speed. (See figure 5.) There has to be a balance, too, between value and speed. If you transform too quickly

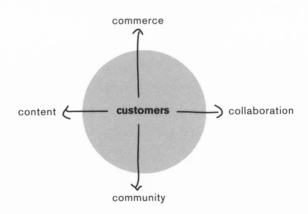

figure 4

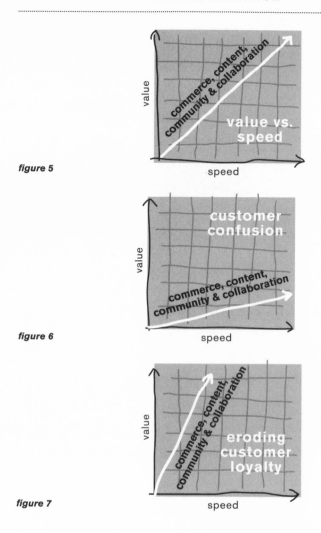

figure 5

figure 6

figure 7

in any of the four "C" areas without a commensurate increase in value, you risk creating customer confusion. (See figure 6.)

On the other hand, if you focus too much on value and not enough on speed, then you risk eroding customer loyalty. (See figure 7.)

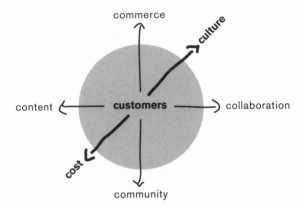

figure 8

There's another aspect to digital transformation that, unfortunately, often gets short shrift. We call these the two small "c"s. They are:

☐ cost and

☐ culture.

Companies too often make the decision to create, deploy and manage their e-business ventures in-house or outside before they consider the cost-and-culture issue. (See figure 8.)

This is a key consideration that may swing the decision one way or another. For example, your decision to keep the e-business initiative inside may be based on its being a "natural" technology for your business. But the costs incurred and cultural changes required may dictate going outside for the incubation period.

There's another key factor to consider only after dealing with the issues of value and speed. That's technology. Here again, there's a danger in doing everything else right and then thinking about technology as a supporting function rather than an enabling function. More than one e-business venture has crashed and burned because it adopted the wrong technology and could not scale or otherwise handle an unanticipated influx of activity. "For the first time in the history of modern business, technology has moved from being a tool to being a determinant of business strategy," says Vinod Khosla, a general partner at venture capital firm Kleiner Perkins Caufield & Byers. "Technology is the principal driver of business strategy," he continues. "This is the most fundamental transformation that has gone on."

> "Technology is the principal driver of business strategy. This is the most fundamental transformation that has gone on."
>
> —Vinod Khosla
> General Partner
> Kleiner Perkins
> Caufield & Byers

In e-business, you had better not trust your projections of resources required. First of all, they are wrong. While in some cases they may only be wrong by a factor of two, in others they could be wrong by a factor of ten. Pick a technology that will cover your imprecision, even if you're off by an order of magnitude.

YOUR BUSINESS NERVOUS SYSTEM

Another way to look at digital transformation is that it's creating the nervous system of your business. It's a good thing that when you touch a hot surface, for example, your reflexes pull your hand away well before your brain registers that you've been burned. If the decision to pull away awaited your sensation of pain, the damage to your skin would be much worse. A champion tennis player's reflexes are often the difference between getting to the ball in time or a fraction of a second too late. Clearly, the movements are reflexive rather than conscious. In a similar way, if you've executed your digital transformation effectively, it too may have reflexes that can initiate action before a slower analysis raises a red or green flag.

Noted neurologist and Stanford University professor Dr. Lawrence Steinman tells us that our nervous systems are very adaptive. As the brain encounters new information, it begins building new synaptic pathways. If the same information is encountered a few more times, the pathways become permanent, that is, the information is "learned." Steinman finds the idea of an e-business infrastructure that is also adaptive to be an interesting concept — one that can adapt based on changing business dynamics. We often hear about business systems that can be adapted to keep pace with change. How about a business system that can change itself?

YOU CAN'T ESCAPE CHANGE

Even where e-business seems an obvious fit, its adoption will require changes in technology, processes and people. John Chambers, president and chief executive officer of Cisco Systems, is the company's e-business leader and champion. He readily admits that, as Cisco progressed along its digital transformation path, it affected how he and everyone else at Cisco worked. "The majority of our employee transactions, including applying to Cisco, changing benefits plans, submitting travel expenses and more, are handled via the Web," says Chambers. "In short, it's changed how everybody in the company has worked — from the president all the way down to the individual contributor in engineering, the manufacturing shop floor and our sales support operation."

Here we see how Cisco's digital transformation affected its community, and specifically, its customers. In fact, Cisco's digital transformation affected all four "C"s. It has changed the rules of partnerships and created a virtual manufacturing entity by closely integrating its manufacturing partners into its e-business system (community and collaboration). Its customer-support system provides a great deal of information online (content), and as noted, Cisco sells over $1 billion in products per month online (commerce).

We are not implying that you have to replace the people within your organization. What you must do is teach them how to adapt. If you succeed in building an organization that sees chaos as opportunity and change as a constant, then you will have an organization that can adapt to anything that comes along. No one would describe GE's Jack Welch as a radical, yet what he's accomplished at GE since the early 1980s has been revolutionary. In large part, Welch's success came from his empowering his people, allowing them to embrace change. GE had suffered from what Vinod Khosla calls "the gravitational pull of the organization." Welch gave his people permission to adapt, and that's how they achieved the necessary "escape velocity."

It is fair to say that no two digital transformations are exactly alike, because no two companies are identical. There are shaping factors associated with digital transformation. Customers, on one end, are telling you how they want to be engaged. That, in turn, will shape the four "C"s in one way. Suppliers, on the other end, will have their preferences, too. Typically, these will be different shaping factors, having an altogether different influence upon the four "C"s. This is an area of inherent imprecision, and you will likely be forced to go through some iterations before finding a best-fit solution.

EMBRACING CHANGE

> **"If you're going to go e-business, understand how it expands your market presence while it cannibalizes your existing channels. Optimize for that, rather than reacting to it."**
>
> —Roger Siboni
> CEO
> E.piphany

"It is difficult to get any company to change, especially companies that are successful," says Cisco's CEO. Brick-and-mortar companies planning to join the e-business revolution must be prepared for major changes to their current business practices. If there are few changes, then something must be wrong.

A profound commitment to e-business means you must be prepared to change not just one thing, but everything. And that's a scary proposition. We did say you would need to be courageous, didn't we? And innovative, too?

First of all, there will be changes to your existing business processes, and innovative changes to your business model may well do away with some existing processes altogether.

For example, the companies that elect to hand off some of their back-office functions to a FedEx or an Ingram Micro should then alter the business processes associated with those functions (collaboration). Your e-business will certainly affect your current channel structure, too. Be prepared to realign your channel strategy to minimize conflict and redundancies. Says E.piphany CEO Roger Siboni, "If you're going to go e-business, understand how it expands your market presence while it cannibalizes your existing channels. Optimize for that, rather than reacting to it."

One of the hallmarks of successful e-business is integration of the value chain. Instead of keeping all your cards close to your vest, share some of what you're holding with your value-chain partners. It isn't a zero-sum game where your win is a value-chain partner's loss. It can be a win-win game where the whole value chain shares information and objectives (collaboration, community, content and commerce).

ENHANCED CUSTOMER INTERACTION

The customer is at the center of digital transformation. A lot has been written and said about the huge business paradigm shift that has followed in the wake of the Web. Some, for example, argue that the concept of customer relationship marketing (CRM) is a misplaced idea in the context of e-business. "You don't manage the customers, they manage you," says Cisco's Amir Hartman. Yet at the same time, E.piphany, which specializes in e-business CRM, enjoys an astounding market valuation.

"The issue about who manages whom is semantics," says Siboni. To illustrate, he describes some of E.piphany's work with American Airlines. "The airline wants to make it easier for customers to buy tickets on the Net. And they're doing that, already. We're helping them understand more about each customer that comes to the site — who they are, how much they fly, from where to where and so on. The idea is to achieve a single view of the customer that takes into account their travel history with American, loops in the frequent flier point program, integrates travel partners and does it in real time. There's nothing manipulative about that. We're [American Airlines and customers] managing each other."

We believe you need to have an internal focus aimed at actually enhancing customer interaction. Amazon.com, for example, provides immediate feedback to its customers. Within seconds of purchasing a book, a CD, or a toy, customers receive e-mail confirmation of the orders and the shipping schedules. Customers also receive subsequent e-mail notices when the orders have been shipped. In addition, when someone orders a book, Amazon.com provides a list of related books that others who purchased the same book have also ordered. It's all done in a very soft-pedaled and non-offensive way.

For Amazon.com, a born-on-the-Web company, this is the only way it has been doing business. For brick-and-mortar bookstores, though, an Amazon-like e-business effort involves practices that are foreign to physical bookstores. When was the last time you purchased a book at a bookstore and had the cashier tell you the names of four or five related books that you might find interesting?

TRANSFORM FOR EFFICIENCIES, NOT PIZZAZZ

Your digital transformation is far better served by looking for added efficiency than for amusement value. Sure, the cow on the Ben & Jerry's Web site did say "moo." And the Levi's Web site was considered "ultra-cool." But Levi's abandoned its Web efforts, so, obviously, "cool" didn't help sell enough jeans.

The media is preoccupied with Internet "cool." You should not be. Check out the Cisco, Intel or Hewlett-Packard Web sites. They are designed to get you the information you're looking for with minimal clicks in minimal time. Remember, both Cisco and Intel are racking up $1 billion a month and Cisco has slashed more than $800 million in operating costs as a result of putting virtually everything online. And neither Web site could be described as particularly "cool." Even the most successful b2c Web sites are far more functional than "cool."

GIVE TRANSFORMATION POWER TO THE FUNCTIONS

Who should be making transformation decisions? Should the CIO be responsible for all of it? Should marketing be setting business imperatives for manufacturing? Should IT be doing it for sales? We don't think so. Those who excel at e-business, in most cases, have let people managing those functions make their own decisions. In fact, Cisco's Pete Solvik (the CIO) goes one better. The business unit making an e-business request has to fund the project. This alleviates the need for a blanket IT budget to fund a collection of projects. It also gives each business unit a much greater vested interest in the scope, costs and schedules for their projects.

The Four "C"s of Digital Transformation

☐ Commerce

☐ Content

☐ Community

☐ Collaboration

CHAPTER 4

First-Mover Advantages and New Business Models

In the old days, those who were fast to market had the advantages of momentum and higher margins. Those who followed generally didn't. Today, the first-movers walk away with all the marbles. Here's why.

NO MORE MARKET ADOPTION SEQUENCE

In the pre-Web days, every product was supposed to move through a predictable market adoption sequence. First, early adopters got the ball rolling. Then the early majority came in. At this point the product demand rises most rapidly and return-on-investment is typically highest. Once the majority begins adopting, the product volumes begin to flatten, then turn downward. Finally, the late adopters and laggards follow, buying the product at commodity price levels, as sales volumes sink back toward the X axis. (See figure 9.)

In that scenario, early movers reaped the early adopter margins and volumes, but companies just getting into the market during that phase could still conceivably make profits through very efficient manufacturing. During the late-adopter and laggard phases, most of the early movers had already moved on, leaving the remaining demand to be fulfilled by those companies set up to earn money on commodity-priced products.

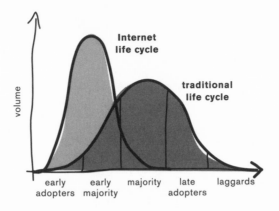

figure 9

The time frame involved in the market adoption sequence had grown shorter, giving the advantage to companies who were fleet of foot. But the Internet-based life cycle has created a "winner-take-all" scenario. In this situation, the adoption curve rises quickly and steeply, then falls quickly and steeply. If you're not on the early part of the rising side, you're nowhere.

What that means for you is that there's no percentage in trying to out-Amazon Amazon. You have to do something different to excel. You have to write new rules of the game that force those who follow you to cede your space to you, while trying to find their own differentiators. There are no successful also-rans in e-business.

YOU'VE GOT TO "THINK DIFFERENT"

When you're working up a vision for your e-business crusade, the word you should keep in the front of your mind is "different." And remember, that differentiation can be fleeting.

Consider the sale of music online. First-movers, like CDNow.com, adopted a business model similar to Amazon's. Customers could order, online, from a large and diverse inventory of music CDs. The prices were typically lower than those at brick-and-mortar music stores, even with the delivery charges. The tradeoff, of course, was the loss of instant gratification.

Along came a competitor who thought "different." There was no distinction in trying to be another CDNow, competing on the basis of price. Instead, this competitor created a new value offering — customized CDs. Customers could specify only the tracks they wanted. That had appeal to CD buyers who chafed at the idea of having to buy all the tracks in order to hear just the few they really liked. In fact, they were willing to pay a premium for that customization.

> You have to write new rules of the game that force those who follow you to cede your space to you, while trying to find their own differentiators. There are no successful also-rans in e-business.

CDNow and its first-mover cohorts were forced to offer customized CDs, too. But the new competitor had the first-mover advantage in that custom-CD space.

Unlike software, which can be easily downloaded, music on CDs is a very data-intensive medium. It used to take several hours, for example, to download a typical CD in native format. But MPEG Layer 3 audio compression technology (MP3) provides 12-to-1 data reduction without objectionable degradation of music quality. With it, a CD that once took four hours to download can now be downloaded in 20 minutes. That's why music has become a product that can be readily delivered online. There are, of course, legal issues to be wrangled with and sorted out, but this genie is out of the bottle. And now there is a way for an online music company to provide convenience, low prices and nearly instant gratification.

DELIVERING FUNCTION WITHOUT THE FORM CAN BE A FIRST-MOVER STRATEGY

You can be a first-mover without having to invent something new. Just look for a way to deliver it differently. For example, another way to look at what the MP3-based music sites are delivering is function without the form, that is, music without the CD or cassette tape. And there are lots of positive economic implications when a company does this.

DELIVERING FUNCTION WITHOUT FORM

When FedEx partners with National Semiconductor to become its picking, packing and shipping arm, it is providing delivery to National. Thus, National doesn't have to deal with boxes, bubble pack and tape. Again, this is function separated from form.

There are many opportunities in e-business to provide this separation, exploit economies of scale, and offer differentiated services with greater convenience and lower cost.

DIAGNOSTIC FUNCTION
WITHOUT FORM

A few years ago, HP Labs was toying with the idea of a computer service station. An HP service person located in Cupertino, California would be able to download software to a customer in New York, for example, and diagnose the customer's computer problem remotely, in real time.

Now, let's take that idea a bit further. Today, when you have a problem with Windows 98, you can call a phone number and interact with a real person. He tells you to reboot, and you reboot. He tells you to select "start," then "run," then type in "msconfig." So you do that. He then walks you through a sequence of steps, asking you questions along the way. Depending upon the nature of the problem, the process can take a long time to complete.

Suppose you could log onto a Web site, and sit back while a Web site-resident troubleshooting application took control of your computer and raced through all those same manual steps. You could be doing other work at the same time, while your computer was handling diagnosis and troubleshooting. It's just a variation on the theme of separating function from form, with the form, in this case, being your participation in the repair process.

CRM FUNCTION WITHOUT FORM

In another instance of function separated from form, the company Rainmaker offers eCRM services to software and other high-technology companies. Rainmaker does not sell hardware, software, or CRM consulting. What it does is partner with its clients and handle their CRM needs remotely. To the client and its customers, Rainmaker is completely transparent. In fact, Rainmaker has innovated in another way, as well. Unlike other marketing groups that charge their clients for activity (e.g. the number of phone calls), Rainmaker does not charge its clients anything. Its business model is based on using its clients' databases to find opportunities to do business. These include sales of upgrades, subscriptions, support services and education services.

Rainmaker collects the fees for these new sales, then deducts its percentage and sends the balance to the client. Like FedEx and Ingram Micro, Rainmaker also provides its clients with back-office services such as order processing, accounts receivable, fulfillment and inventory management. The function is CRM without the costs, integration and training efforts usually associated with it.

SOFTWARE APPLICATIONS FUNCTION WITHOUT FORM

Finally, here is a different slant on the idea of separating form and function. Today, software companies sell you an application, and usually some support services to go along with it. Then, over time, they have to deal with managing different versions of the software, because customers do not upgrade at the same time.

Suppose that, instead of selling you software, an entity sold you access to software, much akin to today's ISP selling you access to the Internet. The application would, in fact, be resident on a server or servers at the host's site. You would pay a monthly, quarterly or annual fee that would be recurring, but would be far lower than the cost of the software itself.

The entities that provide this service are called application service providers (ASPs). They hope to become new intermediaries between customers and software companies. And all of their customers would have access to the latest upgrades, because the master software would always be current. For the software companies, if such a business model takes off (and many market analysts are predicting it will take off in a very big way), it would make their life a lot easier, because they would only have to support one version instead of two or three. They would have to support only the ASPs who would, in turn, support the software end-users.

The Net is the enabling technology behind ASPs. Without the Internet, it couldn't work. To be sure, there are some flies in the ointment here. In order for the software end-users to be satisfied with performance, key parts of the application would have to be resident in their machines. Just think about the frustration if you had to download all of Microsoft Word every time you wanted to create a document. And that problem underscores another problem. With tens of megabytes of RAM and gigabytes of storage to play with on today's desktop machines, software developers have not been motivated to produce "thin" (i.e., smaller-sized) applications.

That is the reason for the fragmentation of the solution: some code on the user's system, the rest of the code on the ASP's server.

But being able to pay for an expensive ERP application on a much lower monthly basis, for example, is an appealing proposition to mid-size and smaller companies. As such, it would expand the software companies' markets as well as that of the ASPs. And, if it does take off on a grand scale, it will mean significantly increased sales of network infrastructure equipment — servers, routers, switches and so on. It is also creating an opportunity for consulting groups to help ASPs develop their businesses and act as integrators for customers, such as the new Qwest/KPMG venture — Qwest CyberSolutions.

The ASP business is one example of using the characteristics of e-business to create a new value proposition, based on new relationships with customers (the software end-users) and suppliers (the software companies).

THE MEGAEXCHANGE – A NEW BUSINESS MODEL

The megaexchange is taking advantage of the Web's ability to support "many-to-many," two-way connectivity and communications. There are already several e-businesses whose vision is to create markets of b2b sellers and buyers.

For example, eSteel.com is an online marketplace for the buying and selling of steel products. It is a neutral participant that has no ownership of any products bought or sold through its systems. In addition to being an e-venue for buying and selling steel products, eSteel.com provides its members with industry information. Suppliers use eSteel.com to expand their market reach and grow their customer bases, all while reducing their transaction costs. At the same time, it helps buyers increase their supplier bases, find better prices and lower their purchasing costs.

VerticalNet.com supports several market communities, each representing a different industry. VerticalNet, like eSteel, offers an online marketplace and industry content. It also has a "career center," for those needing to fill positions and those looking for positions to fill. It was originally launched as Water Online, in 1995, and has since grown to include more than 55 vertical communities.

Chemdex.com is a third example of a megaexchange, in this case focusing on life sciences. Like the others, it establishes a marketplace for buying and selling of products.

Some large corporations are creating their own megaexchanges, too. Ford Motor Company and Oracle announced the formation of AutoXchange, an automotive e-business integrated supply chain to be created and run by a joint venture. The idea, here, is to transform Ford's $80 billion in annual purchasing transactions with its 30,000-plus suppliers by creating a $300 billion extended supply chain. The objective is to reduce Ford's purchasing costs while increasing its operating efficiencies.

A PATENTED COMMERCE MODEL

Priceline.com changed the rules of the game and achieved first-mover advantage. Before Priceline.com, there was the concept of manufacturer's suggested retail price (MSRP). Remember? That was back in the days of information asymmetry, linear supply chains, clear industry boundaries, multi-year product lifecycles and marketing plans.

Priceline.com's founders decided to change the rules. Every industry has the problem of excess inventory — even the so-called "just-in-time" manufacturers. (Don't let them kid you.) Airlines have unsold seats on flights, hotels have unoccupied rooms, groceries have too many half-gallon cartons of milk and car rental agencies have cars sitting on their lots.

The problem was how to sell the excess inventory, gain incremental revenues and profits, all without cannibalizing regular retail pricing. The solution, in short, was Priceline.com's vision. It wasn't about being an aggregator, or an online auction company. It was something new and different. In fact, Priceline.com received a patent for its buyer-driven commerce model.

Priceline.com's Web site is deceptively simple. For example, you register, giving Priceline.com your credit card information, then select an airline embarkation and destination, date and acceptable time range. After that, you enter how much you would be willing to pay for that ticket. You can't choose your airline, or the number of intermediate stops. But if Priceline.com finds an airline willing to take your deal, you just bought yourself a ticket.

It works the same way for hotel rooms, rental cars, long-distance calling rates, and now groceries. In fact, Priceline.com's grocery service — WebHouse Club — is a raging success, according to Priceline.com president and COO Dan Schulman. "In the first 12 weeks after we launched it, we got over 125,000 grocery customers in New York City," says Schulman, "and 80 percent were repeat customers."

That's a particularly impressive statistic when you consider that the average grocery customer shops 75 times per year, compared with the average leisure airline ticket buyer who flies about twice a year. Even more impressive is the fact that among all New York City households — those that are online, offline, and cutting across all socioeconomic strata — two percent are using Priceline.com to grocery shop. "It is far and away our fastest Priceline.com startup," Schulman asserts. "And through WebHouse, Priceline.com has become the number one online seller of groceries."

By changing the rules in several different areas, Priceline.com has achieved very noteworthy results. For example, the airlines in its ticketing program all grew at faster rates than those that were not in it. "We started with two airlines and sold 43 tickets the first day — at substantial loss — but now we've proven our concept and all the airlines have become part of our program," Schulman says. Priceline.com, launched in April 1998, is today driving about four percent of all leisure airline ticket-sales traffic. The company expects to end the year 2000 with revenues in excess of $1 billion. And it will have moved into the Fortune 1000 in less than two-and-a-half years.

FIRST AND DIFFERENT

The preceding examples are meant to reinforce the following points. The Web is not kind to followers. You must strive to be number one or two in your category. And you become number one or two by differentiating your business and providing your customers with a valuable relationship. Being number one or two, of course, does not guarantee you'll be profitable. That's where innovative business practices, operational efficiency and collaboration come in. But if you're not a leader in your e-business market category, the other benefits may be moot.

Priceline.com is today driving about four percent of all leisure airline ticket-sales traffic. The company expects to end the year 2000 with revenues in excess of $1 billion. And it will have moved into the Fortune 1000 in less than two-and-a-half years.

CHAPTER 5

The b2b Challenges

In the old B.W. (before Web) days, the name of the b2b game was to beat your competitor at his own game. In those days, the lines of demarcation between suppliers, manufacturers, distributors, competitors and customers were solid and black. But not today.

The structure of an industry — its infrastructure — was typically decades old and immutable. That's not the case anymore. Today's winners don't play by the rules of the game, they change them. They form strategic partnerships. They move up the food chain, creating new value and new business models.

Let's examine a few companies that used digital transformation to achieve competitive advantages, operational efficiencies, agility and flexibility.

CREATING A NEW PARTNERSHIP MODEL

There was a time when partnerships and alliances were a move of desperation. For example, when companies didn't have, or couldn't develop, the core competencies they knew they would need for their businesses, they looked for partners and allies that did. In the biotechnology industry, startup companies might develop an innovative product, but typically would have to ally with a large pharmaceuticals company in order to distribute it.

However, what was a move of necessity less than a decade ago is a critical success factor today. Partnerships are crucial, but forging good ones, fast enough, is more art than science.

We won't rehash Cisco's history of accomplishments here. Suffice it to say that the company's track record is nothing short of inspiring. From 1990, when it went public, its revenues grew from $69 million to more than $12.2 billion in fiscal 1999. For our purposes, though, what is really significant about the Cisco story is how its use of the Internet helped it to write new rules for partnerships, and in so doing, to emerge as one of the biggest and best e-businesses on the planet.

First, let's look at Cisco's business. It's the leading provider of network access equipment. The list includes network hardware, network software, design and implementation expertise, plus technical support. The company essentially serves three markets: enterprises, service providers and small- to medium-sized businesses.

Its current business structure evolved over a six-phase period. In phase one, Cisco was a one-product company selling network routers. In phase two, it created a range of products, including switches and data access points. In the third phase, the company provided end-to-end products that drove messaging systems from the sender right through to the receiver. During this phase, the company increasingly focused on quality of service, cost reductions and business process reengineering.

In phase four, Cisco chose to lead the integration of voice, data and video, and the company realized that only the Internet could provide the degree of integration it would demand.

CISCO'S INTERNET BUSINESS SOLUTIONS GROUP

In the fifth phase, Cisco created the Internet Business Solutions Group (IBSG) to research and develop online applications that could be used to drive business processes, such as budgeting, accounting, preparation of financial reports, and marketing forecasts. It was at this stage that Cisco turned to business partnerships to diversify its range of products and services. Consequently, phase six is marked by Cisco's migration to business partnerships as the solution for making its vision a reality.

A key factor in creating IBSG was Cisco recognizing that business systems could be designed on a modular basis. As a result, you could choose the best software applications for any particular business and put them into service incrementally. Business applications hosted on the Internet — such as accounting or employee management packages — can provide integrated delivery for partnerships, allowing them to establish one-stop shops in-house. Because all this is Internet-based, an integrated business and all its administrative systems can be set up practically overnight. That's a dramatic change to the partnership game rules.

Cisco's mission is to accelerate the adoption of Internet business solutions through alliances and the creation of what they call Internet "ecosystems" in markets with great potential. By integrating horizontally, Cisco can participate in all aspects of the Internet business. With this approach, Cisco can work with the best in each segment, creating segment-level "ecosystems" in which all of the participants have access to a server and all of the relevant information.

Cisco created the IBSG service essentially to form knowledge networks with its partners. This group is comprised of a range of Cisco's application vendors and systems-integration consulting firms. IBSG helps these vendors do their parts in implementing Web-based solutions.

Through the IBSG's knowledge transfer program, Cisco shares with these partners best practices about its own Internet-based business methods and applications. In turn, these partners use Cisco as their strategic networking vendor for deploying Internet business solutions. They also employ Cisco methods within their own consulting practice groups and services offerings.

The partners transfer knowledge through face-to-face customer advisory sessions, seminars sponsored by multiple vendors and training sessions on Internet-based solutions. In addition, the group prepares detailed case studies, white papers, reference network architectures and best practice recommendations. These are used for implementing

Internet-based applications in areas such as employee services, electronic commerce, customer care and supply-chain management.

This is, without question, a new approach to alliances. Not only does Cisco reap the benefits from partnering, in terms of additional resources and knowledge, it also puts these required resources into the venture, thus ensuring that partners are able to maintain the fast pace required to keep up with the alliance demands.

Agility and flexibility are two of the key benefits of this structure. They give the partnership the ability to add new services and react to market trends in a way that was previously impossible. Cisco makes this possible because it can rapidly develop and deploy services.

For example, Cisco integrates front- and back-office functions through Web-based processes, and the group uses partnership experience to apply core competencies to new areas. Using the Web to repurpose and redeploy core competencies in this way changes the rules of partnering, because it lowers transaction costs and knowledge barriers among the partners, thereby empowering all of them.

Today, Cisco can launch a new business concept practically overnight by creating an alliance of skills and resources between key providers and coordinating them through Internet-based management systems. In changing the rules of partnership, Cisco has definitely changed the game of corporate competition.

CHANGING THE VALUE CHAIN
IN THE "CHIP" BUSINESS

Intel's former chairman, Andy Grove, wrote the book called *Only The Paranoid Survive*. And no company was as vociferous as Intel when it came to its data security. Yet, its changing business requirements made Intel's embrace of e-business — including information exchange over the Web — too beneficial to dismiss.

Today, Intel's e-business operates in more than 46 countries, with over 560 customers, and serves more than 4000 users. But as recently as 1997, Intel was not using the Internet for transactions at all. Its traditional channel model was supplier-centric. The company had sophisticated back-end Enterprise Resource Planning (ERP) systems in place with manual front-end processing. It took a lot of dedicated personnel (called "customer business analysts") to receive and process customer orders.

Again, security was a very critical issue because of the highly competitive and technical nature of Intel's and its customers' businesses. Secure exchange of information was a paramount consideration. In fact, confidential documents were often hand-delivered between Intel and its customers.

Understandably, Intel's costs to manage its business kept growing. By 1997, its business had grown to $25 billion. Also, Intel's customer base had increased to approximately 50,000 worldwide customers. Transaction volumes were huge and Intel's product-mix included thousands of items.

So Intel had to take action. It acted courageously, and it innovated. It changed the way it dealt with every part of its value chain by developing an Internet-based solution.

OBJECTIVES

Intel's primary objective was to do a better job for its customers and shareholders. The original channel model had been supplier-centric, but the new Internet model would focus on the customer.

Intel's expectations included enhanced customer relationships, improved value chain efficiency and inventory management and reduced costs of management.

In addition, Intel hoped to influence a shift toward an Internet economy. By demonstrating the advantages of its own best practices, Intel expected it would have a positive impact on sales of its own products.

INTEL'S NEW MODEL

Intel's new model uses the Internet for a range of different functions along the value chain, including order and transaction processing and technical support. To support the value chain, Intel designed and launched a family of Web sites.

Before they launched the new model, Intel received nearly 75 percent of its direct-customer orders by fax or phone. They processed another 20 percent by using an electronic data interchange (EDI) system. But Intel felt they could handle orders more efficiently by developing a secure Internet-based system for order processing and fulfillment. They knew that would also enable better inventory management for the company and its customers.

Intel changed the way it deals with every part of its value chain by developing an Internet-based solution.

So Intel created a series of non-transactional Web sites to provide its customers with improved product and technical information and Web-based training.

In addition, they developed informational Web sites to give channel, or indirect customers (resellers, integrators, developers), technical information and design help.

Finally, Intel designed a series of Web sites for end-users. (See figure 10.)

Again, these Web sites are non-transactional, but provide consumers with marketing information, new ideas and tools. These Web sites are accessible by everyone.

ACHIEVING THESE OBJECTIVES

Intel already had its governance in place. Its sales and marketing groups were the leaders and drivers of its Internet program. They were responsible for applications development, infrastructure and secure processing. Its planning and logistics groups provided the service interface to customers, because people working on that team have a direct, one-to-

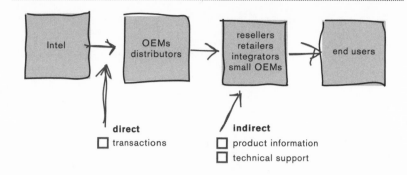

figure 10

one, front-end relationship with Intel's customers. For both development and implementation, this team was responsible for customer services, corporate databases, ERP, planning and order fulfillment.

Information Technology (IT) provided the final input. The IT team was responsible for overall program management, systems integration, marketing and the program's international focus.

Intel developed the program in-house, from end-to-end, because its specialized business processes made it practically impossible to buy an off-the-shelf solution. Initially, Intel expected the "automate" phase of the program to take two years. (See figure 11.)

But this first phase was actually completed in only one year. The key elements were development, deployment and usage.

During the development, the Intel staff did thorough workflow analysis so that they could truly understand their industry's complex value chain. At the same time, they were

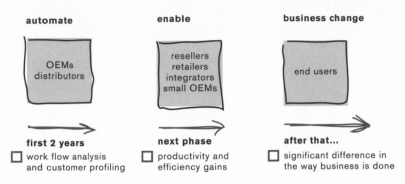

automate

OEMs
distributors

enable

resellers
retailers
integrators
small OEMs

business change

end users

first 2 years
☐ work flow analysis
and customer profiling

next phase
☐ productivity and
efficiency gains

after that...
☐ significant difference in
the way business is done

figure 11

developing the applications and infrastructure to support the model.

Before deploying the program, an Intel team did substantial customer profiling. Afterward, the system was deployed to these customers — the "enable" phase.

For Intel, measuring use of its system is an ongoing process. It collects, collates and analyzes customer feedback, then makes iterative design changes and system updates. The company recognized early on that it was more important to deploy a workable model, and refine it over time, than to try to achieve a perfect model at the outset. Its digital transformation is taking place in carefully deployed phases. When it gets to the "business change" phase, its digital transformation will be essentially complete.

PROGRAM REPORT CARD

Intel's new system offers individual users customized, interactive Web sites. Its customer satisfaction rating is now pegged at 94 percent, overall. The system supports product ordering all day, every day. And by using 128-bit encryption technology, the company has security that even a paranoid CEO would love.

By the second half of 1999, Intel's Internet orders were approximately 50 percent of the total. Overall, direct customers have shifted from ordering by phone and fax to ordering through the Internet. Meanwhile, the number of orders using the proprietary EDI system has remained fairly constant. Intel estimates that it takes 70 percent less time to process a transaction using e-business, so its goal is to have more of its customers adopt the new model.

> **Intel estimates that it takes 70 percent less time to process a transaction using e-business**

The Intel Experience:

☐ It took less time than expected.

☐ It was an iterative process.

☐ Customer satisfaction soared.

☐ Security was preserved.

☐ Transactions took 70 percent less time.

CHANGING THE WAY THEY PURCHASE

Is Microsoft an e-business? "Absolutely," says Peter Boit, their vice-president of e-business solutions. Like Cisco and Intel, Microsoft is using digital transformation to cut costs, increase customer satisfaction, maintain growth and empower employees.

Like most companies, Microsoft had a traditional approach to purchasing. If an employee needed a new computer, she first filled out a purchase request. This paperwork then made its way to a manager who had to approve it. Then, the signed copy "flowed" to the purchasing department. At that point, the purchasing department checked its list of distributors and called for quotes, and the finance department received a request for funds. These papers had to be checked and signed before being returned to the purchasing department. Finally, at the conclusion of this flurry of paper passing, the order was placed.

So how much did this purchase cost Microsoft? In addition to the price of the shipped computer, the process alone added another $60. With an annual purchase of more than 250,000 products totaling around $1.6 billion, that $60 key on the cash register got pushed a lot of times.

Today, when a Microsoft employee needs a new computer, she opens a page on their intranet and clicks on the product. This automatically forwards an e-mail message to her manager. With another click, the manager can approve the request, which is then automatically sent to the SAP supply application, and the order is placed.

The supplier sends a confirmation, ships the computer and sends an electronic invoice to the finance department. If the product is available from the distributor, the employee receives the computer in a matter of days. Before, the process often took weeks. When you shave weeks off of the delivery time, that employee can begin doing his work sooner. That might have been enough of an incentive to make the change, even without the money saved. But the cost of the purchase transaction has dropped to $5 — and that includes the costs associated with managing the new purchasing infrastructure.

It took Microsoft only a few staff-months to build the new purchasing system, yet it saved the company nearly $15 million in its first year of use.

INDIRECT BENEFITS DWARF THE DIRECT BENEFITS

As dramatic as the savings in direct costs are, Microsoft says the indirect benefits are far more valuable. Its employees can now focus their efforts on critical business issues rather than on internal administration. In addition, the new system makes access to information, communication and collaboration easier, which results in better sharing of best business practices and improved decision-making.

> It took Microsoft only a few staff-months to build the new purchasing system, yet it saved the company nearly $15 million in its first year of use.

The digital transformation that Microsoft has undertaken involves more than just automating activities, or putting information online. By implementing the digital nervous system, Microsoft changed the mindset of the corporation. "Greater productivity, greater customer focus, better ideas, greater agility and greater employee satisfaction: All these benefits have come by virtue of changing the way our own employees work," says Boit.

The Microsoft Experience:

☐ Got rid of the latencies

☐ Lowered transaction cost from $60 to $5

☐ Better focus on critical business issues

☐ Many indirect benefits too

Several b2b e-businesses have been enormously successful at fully exploiting the advantages of the Net. They've used it to gain more operational efficiency, to lower operational costs and to create agile partnerships. Both FedEx and Ingram Micro, for example, used their digital transformations to move them further up the food chain. And Cisco is using digital transformation to do virtual manufacturing by closely integrating its manufacturing partners and its own manufacturing facilities.

b2b e-Business Results

☐ Lower latencies

☐ Lower operational costs

☐ Seamless partnerships

☐ Virtual manufacturing

CHAPTER 6

The b2c Challenges

The b2c world has all the same challenges as the b2b world. The b2c companies must shoot for the number one or two position. They must differentiate and innovate. They have to find ways of using the Web to add efficiencies and lower their costs. And they must explore ways of shortening their order-to-delivery cycles, just like any b2b company.

B ut b2c companies, by their very nature, depend more on the Web's overall population for e-commerce than do their b2b counterparts. Using the Web for b2c e-commerce poses a new set of challenges and opportunities for the b2c world. The trick is to rise to the first and exploit the second. And one of the first challenges is letting people know you're there.

"WE'RE HERE"

On Sunday, January 30, 2000, 17 dot.com companies spent an average of $2.2 million dollars for 30-second TV advertisements during the Superbowl. They represented nearly half of all Superbowl advertisers (there were 38). The previous year, there were only two dot.coms in the Superbowl advertising group.

The purpose of these ads was to raise the consciousness of Superbowl viewers about the existence of these Web sites and their companies. That's what interrupt marketing is all about. Get people doing one thing (watching a football game) to stop and do something else (pay attention to your advertising message).

Let's say that out of the umpteen million viewers watching, 1000 of them actually visited one of those Web sites. How much did it cost to drive them there? $2,200 per head! If 10,000 visited, it cost $220 per head. That's a lot of freight to get someone to maybe buy a product that sells for under $20, such as a book or CD. Even if there is a branding "halo" effect, the entire branding and sales process has become increasingly more expensive.

OurBeginnings.com, an Orlando, Florida online stationery supplier, indicated that its Superbowl ad spurred a 550 percent increase in Web activity and a 400 percent increase in sales. But it will be interesting to see if these sales were enough to pay for their $4 million campaign. As Jeff Moulton, an analyst for PC Data, points out, "The real question is whether such sites can sustain these traffic volumes throughout the remainder of the year." Then, too, Pets.com and Lifeminders.com saw a fall in visitor activity by 5 and 13 percent, respectively.

We're not trying to comment on the advisability of such advertising; we're simply pointing out that the cost of driving the right people to the right Web site is going up. In fact, it may be rising in direct proportion to the increase in Web population.

The costs of interrupt marketing (direct mail and advertising) are rising and the effectiveness is waning. Why?

Because people today have an abundance of practically everything except time. And people are getting more and more selective about how they spend their time. Paying attention to interrupt marketing isn't high on their priority lists. The result is a vicious cycle. Advertisers increase the frequency of interrupt marketing in order to try and rise above the noise. But that, in turn, creates even more noise. So, they have to ramp up the frequency, and spend even more just to achieve parity with where they were the last time around.

As we said earlier, e-businesses like Cisco and Intel didn't have to raise the consciousness of people about the existence of their Web sites. Intel does spend on advertising to maintain or enhance its "Intel inside" branding. And Cisco spends money advertising its "Empowering the Internet Generation" branding. But it's unlikely either would think of spending $2.2 million dollars to drive new people to their respective Web sites.

The costs of interrupt marketing (direct mail and advertising) are rising and the effectiveness is waning.

Why?

Because people today have an abundance of practically everything except time.

For b2c companies, the Web's population is a tempting target of opportunity. "Its immediacy is incredibly attractive," Dave Wetherell, CEO of CMGI, points out. "With a mailing list, you're looking at demand and preference profiles that are, on average, 12 months old. With the Web, you can see trends that are only 12 seconds old." Although its focus is primarily b2b, CMGI is building a network of e-business companies that address the Web's unique opportunities in the areas of advertising and marketing. "We believe we can provide greater targeting by tracking what people are interested in without abrogating privacy issues," Wetherell says. "We focus on how recently, how often and how long people visit Web sites. But we never combine this information with users' identities."

WHO'S OUT THERE?

The Internet population has been changing constantly since 1994, not just in number but in demography. Prior to 1994, the Internet was a Unix-oriented, text-dominated network. E-mail was (and still is) the "killer application." But the World Wide Web and Mosaic set off an explosion in Internet popularity, and the world was changed irrevocably.

Web Population More Than Triples in Three Years

In just the last three years the overall Web population is estimated to have grown from about 74 million to 250 million. That's an average growth rate of nearly five million users per month and it continues to accelerate. Keep in mind that no one really knows how many users there are. All projections are based on polling surveys, but, Vint Cerf, senior vice president for Internet architecture and technology at MCI Worldcom, points out that the ratio of users to host names is now about three-to-one. And with about 80 million host names, the latest numbers appear to be consistent with that ratio.

Thus, the total of Internet users worldwide has more than tripled in three years time, with the biggest growth in terms of percentages coming from Asia/Pacific, Europe and South America. But these are just numbers. What do we know of the people behind those numbers?

Online Shopping Is Increasing

According to ActivMedia Research, consumers spent about $66 billion online in 1999. Forty percent of online shoppers bought consumables online. The most popular items were health and cosmetic products, accounting for nearly half ($1.9 billion) of the $3.8 billion spent on consumables.

More People, More Frequently

Based on information from The Pew Research Center for the People & the Press, we know that 41 percent of Americans go online. That is a 300 percent increase since 1995. One-third of Americans use e-mail, three times as many as in 1997. Over 22 million Americans go online every day — that's four times as many as in 1997. On average, these users spend an hour or less on the Internet at any given time. New users see the Web as an entertainment medium, while more experienced users exploit the Web for work, research and other "practical" purposes.

POPULAR MYTHS

So the Web is growing, and its population is younger and more educated. Those are the facts. Now let's take a look at some of the myths.

Hits are a Good Measuring Stick

The number of traffic hits is not a good measure of success. There's no way to correlate the number of hits with sales, market share or branding effectiveness. Hits are nothing more than a "ping" on your home page.

The number of traffic hits is not a good measure of success. There's no way to correlate the number of hits with sales, market share or branding effectiveness. Hits are nothing more than a "ping" on your home page. A strategy based on increasing your hits is a loose-canon strategy that provides you with neither correlation nor causation.

Great Content Leads to Repeat Visits

Great content may (and we emphasize "may") lead to two visits. But, by the second visit, if the content hasn't changed, there will not be a third visit. Unless you can engage visitors and offer them a good reason to return, they won't.

The Secret to Sales Success Is a Secure Server

A secure server may help instill confidence in buyers, but they first have to be sold. And selling is about selling.

Technology merely supports the sale; it has nothing to do with making it.

To Get Traffic to Your Site, You Can Depend on Search Engines and Key Words

Probably the least effective means of getting traffic to your site are search engines and key words. Sure, you can "pay for play" and have key words on Yahoo!, say, drive your Web site to someone's short list. But you have to replicate that cost across all the search-engine sites that you think your prospects might use. This strategy is definitely a case of diminishing, not increasing, returns.

You Need to be Cutting Edge to Succeed

The look-and-feel of your Web site does not have to be cutting edge, but your business model had better be. Your customers appreciate an uncluttered site with clear navigation and easy-to-use features. Animation, background music and other data-intensive window dressings make download times longer and increase the risk of a visitor moving on.

Consider the Web as Just Like Television

This one myth has been responsible for more wasted money and failed efforts than any of the others. The Web is not television. It isn't 200 million viewers selecting from among dozens of channels of pre-defined programming. It isn't people choosing to be passively entertained while being interrupted by commercial messages. It is 200 million users looking for specific information in a field of millions of possible channels. What works for television does not work for the Web.

Many People Are Surfing the Web

The average user visits 100 Web sites, bookmarks 14, then stops surfing. Your odds of being visited by casual Web surfers go down with each influx of new users and new commercial Web sites. Journalists, however, are paid to be aggressive surfers. But don't make the mistake of thinking that a journalist's frequent discovery of new, interesting Web sites is representative of users in general. A lot of Web activity is generated by a relatively small number of users.

> **Remember this: When a visitor leaves your Web site dissatisfied, they never return.**

Experiment Quickly or Be a Loser Later

Remember this: When a visitor leaves your Web site dissatisfied, they never return (emphasis on "never"). In your zeal to experiment quickly, don't do so in a slipshod way. Charles Wang, chairman and CEO of Computer Associates International, Inc. points out that, "Too many Web sites are prototypes that are buggy, vulnerable to hackers and failure-prone. They're put together with paper clips and chewing gum, and that doesn't impress anybody." It is important to experiment quickly, but it is even more important to experiment well.

When you check out the Web sites of popular dot.coms, they are not replete with gimmicky features and cool images. Amazon.com makes it easy to select a product category such as books or music first, then move down to specific items within that category. The business model is easy to discern. You search for a product, put it in your shopping cart, then buy it. No one needs lessons on how to navigate, select and buy products on that Web site.

The eBay Web site is another story. An online auction is a different business model. Visitors must be educated first. eBay seems to do a good job of bringing new visitors up to speed on its auction process. And the value of the service is so compelling to many people that millions of users have made the effort to learn to use it. This is due in no small part to eBay making its Web site far more utilitarian than cool.

ADOPT A HOLISTIC PERSPECTIVE

Just as a b2b company must innovate in order to win at e-business, so must a b2c company. It doesn't work to simply try to extend your brick-and-mortar model through an e-commerce interface.

Look at what happened to Toys"R"Us. They created an e-business entity with an e-commerce Web site to try to capitalize on the impending pre-Christmas demand. If they had truly innovated, they would have saved a lot of transaction cost and been able to deliver the purchased goods on time.

But they didn't. E.piphany's Siboni would not have been surprised, because he says, "Distribution and inventory logistics are the hottest competencies that big e-commerce companies are trying to capture."

Toys"R"Us is used to a business model where consumers come to the store, buy the product, and walk out with it. That's a very different model than one where the product is picked, packed and delivered by mail or truck. Any miscalculation in the new model's order processing, credit validation and fulfillment processes could lead to underestimation of order-to-delivery time. And it did.

Toys"R"Us was banking on its brick-and-mortar inventory to buffer it from short supplies in the face of large demands during the 1999 holiday sales period. And it probably did. But regardless of the reasons why a company is out of stock or misses the December 24th delivery deadline, there's still an unfilled space under that Christmas tree. Disgruntled customers don't care about why it happened.

Toys"R"Us didn't have a problem with people finding its Web site, or ordering products directly from that site. They had a problem making the whole scheme work properly. The e-commerce part of e-business was probably a success. A lot of people ordered toys online from them. But in e-business, e-commerce is just one application. And all of the pieces have to play well together.

DIGITAL TRANSFORMATION FOR b2c COMPANIES

To succeed, it takes no less of a profound commitment to digital transformation on the part of b2c companies than it does for b2b companies. The b2c companies have supply chains and value chains, too. They also have front- and back-office systems. They have lots of opportunities for wringing more efficiency out of business processes, cutting costs and streamlining operations through e-business strategies.

As with b2b companies, a Web-based strategy should integrate all aspects of the business. How do customers order from you now? What is the workflow from order to fulfillment? How will digital transformation inject efficiencies into that model? How do suppliers know when and what products to replenish? Is there a way to reduce the lag by sharing order information in real time?

From all indications, Wal-Mart's current digital transformation is going far beyond e-commerce. It will enable Wal-Mart to achieve even greater efficiencies, reduce latencies, manage inventory more effectively and lower operating costs. All that, in turn, will enable Wal-Mart to reduce prices, become even more competitive and achieve higher customer satisfaction, while preserving or increasing its operating margins. And all this from a brick-and-mortar company.

FORGET THE LEVEL PLAYING FIELD

The belief that somehow being on the Net will enable a new, small company to achieve the same visibility, trust and credibility of a much larger, better-known competitor is patently false. Such beliefs are fanned by the name-recognition successes of Amazon.com and eBay.

> **Though the Web environment may be a new playing field, it is anything but level. There are the number one and number two players in each category, and then everyone else.**

But it wasn't the Net that gave them their advantages, it was their vision, innovation and excellent execution. Amazon.com didn't have a level playing field when it chose to compete with Barnes & Noble, Crown and Borders. Amazon.com used the Net to create a new playing field. And it had first-mover advantage, substantial financing and novelty in its favor.

By the way, all of those advantages do not guarantee a profitable business. In its latest financial disclosure, Amazon.com posted higher losses than Wall Street anticipated. But the silver lining was news that its book operation had finally gone from red to black. This is an indication that, for that particular division, Amazon.com is beginning to balance its marketing and operational costs against volumes and gross profit margins.

Though the Web environment may be a new playing field, it is anything but level. There are the number one and number two players in each category, and then everyone else. As we said earlier, the first challenge is letting people know you're there. And that challenge isn't for the faint of heart or shallow of pocket.

A Web user today has no Web directory listings to identify Web sites and companies that fall into various categories. By comparison, a person moving to a new geographic location could turn to the local telephone directory's yellow pages and find a comprehensive and categorical listing of every local company that has a commercial telephone line. But there is no such analog, as yet, for the Web.

For one thing, what does "local" mean in Web terms? For another, which entity controls a Web site's presence on the Web? How useful would it be to Web users to have a directory that displays thousands of URLs for each category or subcategory? And what should those categories be?

In the absence of some kind of directory solution, companies and their Web sites must each find their own ways of letting people know they are there. And while they struggle, the problem gets worse.

So, the egalitarian ideal of a medium that could equalize the presence of a national sporting goods company and a small, local sporting goods shop has not materialized in today's Web. If anything, it is harder for that local sporting goods shop to compete on the Web than it is to compete on Main Street.

THE SPLIT-PERSONALITY WEB

The fantasy of a mom-and-pop e-business is just that: fantasy. You're lulled into a sense of simplicity, because it is so easy to get a Web site up. There are plenty of budding Web developers who will build you one for as little as $100. And there are plenty of ISPs who will host that Web site for a few hundred dollars a year.

But we're talking about a Web site, not an e-business. Sure, there is the odd story about one small business' Web site that is producing thousands of dollars in increased revenues per year. The Web's global reach makes some businesses possible that could never exist with local constraints.

"In the early days of Excite, there was someone looking for a guitar for lepers," says Vinod Khosla, of Kleiner Perkins Caufield & Byers, during an interview for this book. "On a global scale, one could imagine enough business volume for a company that designs guitars for lepers. But in any one location, such a company would never fly."

There are certainly opportunities for small businesses that make specialty products with appeal to an existing community of interest. But we're talking about the very lowest end of the niche-marketing spectrum, here. We're not talking about companies that are seeing tens of millions of dollars of revenues from online sales.

What's emerging, then, are two Webs. Web #1 can support boutique businesses with very specialized products and a narrow base of customers. These small businesses market, typically, through word of mouth on COIN bulletin boards. They do one-to-one marketing the old-fashioned way — personally.

Web #2 can support large b2b and b2c businesses earning millions to billions of dollars of revenues per month. This is the Web where it takes millions of dollars to drive enough visitors to your business Web site. And this is the Web that enables new value creation and innovative business models.

For companies that fit somewhere between these two extremes, the Web may not be a good marketing and sales channel, and business scale may not be large enough to justify the cost of attaining e-business efficiencies. Contrary to what some pundits claim, the Web is not for every company, and e-business may not be the best solution.

But for b2c companies that take a holistic view of their businesses and a realistic view of the Web, opportunities do exist. Their challenges are to:

☐ drive the right people to your Web site

☐ offer customers a more valuable relationship

☐ make your operations more efficient

☐ look for opportunities to partner more effectively.

b2c e-Business Potential

☐ Expanded customer base

☐ Greater operational efficiency

☐ Enhanced one-to-one marketing

☐ Greater supply-chain efficiency

CHAPTER 7

Do It In-House or Spin It Off?

Whenever an existing brick-and-mortar company adopts "e-business," they grapple with the issue of whether to fold it under the parent corporation or to spin it off as an autonomous entity. There are examples of both options, to be sure, but what is the criteria for deciding to go one way or the other?

Bank One, for example, chose to create WingspanBank.com as its online e-bank rather than doing it as Bank One. Toys"R"Us, on the other hand, decided to keep things all under one umbrella.

There's no set-in-stone rule for when to do either one. But there is food for thought in a pre-Web concept.

A NEW SPIN ON A
PRE-WEB CONCEPT

In 1997 Clayton Christensen wrote *The Innovator's Dilemma*. Although the book was published in 1997, it wasn't about the Internet or e-business. It was about well-managed companies failing to make the cut as their industries were transformed by new technologies. Does that sound familiar? His diverse examples include disk drive manufacturers, excavation tool manufacturers, department stores and computer makers.

What prompted his research was why seemingly well-managed companies, apparently doing everything right, all tended to miss the boat when their industries were assaulted by disruptive technologies. For example, all of the makers of 8-inch hard disk drives failed to be major players when the industry shifted to the smaller 5 1/4-inch form factor. The makers of cable-activated excavation equipment failed to make the A List when the industry shifted to hydraulics. Sears and Montgomery Ward were unable to beat back the onslaught of the Kmarts and the Wal-Marts. None of the leaders in the minicomputer market ended up as leaders in the PC market. And the erstwhile kings of that PC market have been challenged by the PC e-business of Dell Computer.

> **"For a discount brokerage house, like Ameritrade or Charles Schwab, e-business is definitely a sustaining technology. But for the old-line brokers such as Merrill-Lynch, it is disruptive."**
>
> –Clayton Christensen
> Author
> *The Innovator's Dilemma*

IT WASN'T BAD MANAGEMENT

At first these failures were attributed to complacency, executives with "tired blood," in-bred management and all manner of human error. But Christensen found that, on the contrary, these companies failed precisely because their management teams were very good at doing exactly what they were supposed to be doing. The problem was that the tried-and-true formulas for success were simply not applicable to dealing with disruptive technologies.

Disruptive technologies are those that are different than

a company's mainstream technology and that have little or no appeal to its customer base, at present. For example, the smaller form-factor disk drives required significant retooling and technology changes and were not of interest to the customers buying the larger form-factor drives. In contrast, sustaining technologies are those that are natural progressions for a company. Again, using disk drives as the example, it was a sustaining technology for companies making drives of a particular size to invest in advanced media and head technologies that made those drives higher-performance and higher-capacity.

In every case that Christensen explored, the problem stemmed from trying to combine a mainstream strategy and disruptive-technology strategy under the same umbrella. Only one company had actually succeeded, and it admitted that the achievement involved great pain. However, those who chose to explore disruptive technologies by acquiring or starting an autonomous entity were able to "eat their own lunch," rather than watching someone else eat it, instead.

THE WEB AS A DISRUPTIVE TECHNOLOGY

Although as we mentioned, Christensen's work did not touch upon the Web, digital transformation or e-business, we saw in his work a new way to think about digital transformation. In helping companies to decide whether to do it in-house or spin the effort off, we felt that it was important to explore whether e-business, itself, could be viewed as sustaining or disruptive. So, we asked Christensen if he agreed that for some companies e-business is a sustaining technology, while for others it could be considered disruptive. He agreed emphatically. "For a discount brokerage house, like Ameritrade or Charles Schwab, e-business is definitely a sustaining technology. But for the traditional brokers, it is disruptive," says Christensen.

It turns out that the market incumbents had no problem adapting sustaining technologies to the parent business. In fact, regarding how they fared, it often didn't matter whether those incumbents were early movers or not. The incumbents who were relatively late in switching from ferrite read/write disk-drive heads to thin-film heads appeared to be at no strategic disadvantage in terms of market position, product performance and margins, for example. Schwab was not the first discount brokerage to adopt e-business, but that didn't prevent it from garnering a leading position.

The problem with disruptive technologies arises because they are not palatable to these companies' mainstream markets. In fact, a disruptive technology may be so new there may not be an apparent market in certain cases. Therefore, managers who are used to extrapolating product sales from existing graphs of total available markets, price/performance targets and predictable applications are often at a loss as to how to plan and manage a disruptive-technology endeavor. And rightly so, says Christensen. So imagine a conventional brokerage house trying to adapt to an e-business environment.

IS e-BUSINESS DISRUPTIVE FOR SECURITIES BROKERS?

Disruptive technologies are usually taken to market by newcomers whose expectations are much more in line with emerging market realities and returns on investment (eTrade, for example). For a while, then, the mainstream market is barely affected by the disruptive technology. Ultimately, though, the disruptive technology advances to a point where the mainstream market is ready to embrace it. And that's when the incumbents begin to see the handwriting on the wall.

The traditional brokerage houses were first confronted by the disruptive technology of discount brokering. Names like Ameritrade and Charles Schwab were soon associated with this new type of trading model. For Ameritrade and Schwab, the Web was a natural extension — a sustaining technology — for their discount-brokerage business models. For the full-service brokers, both discount services and the Web were disruptive technologies. And, as Christensen would have predicted, none of the traditional brokers are number one or two in the e-business space.

The e-business brokerages' markets were initially different from those of the full-service brokers. The two technologies — full-service and e-business discount — appeared to co-exist, with only tangential confrontation. But not anymore. Trading securities online has achieved the necessary credibility, security and convenience to be acceptable to mainstream securities buyers.

IS e-BUSINESS DISRUPTIVE FOR TRAVEL AGENCIES?

Consider brick-and-mortar travel agencies. Whether a local agency or part of a chain, the business model was predicated on trust. The customer trusted the agent to give them the best itinerary for the best price, because most customers were not in possession of an *Official Airline Guide* (OAG). This is a classic case of what Amir Hartman and John Sifonis would describe as an "asymmetric information" situation. Customers had no way of knowing how comprehensive the agent's flight databases were. Before the airlines cut back on travel agency commissions, it cost consumers no more for the agent's services than it would if they bought the ticket at an airline ticket counter.

After the change in commissions, though, travel agencies began charging their customers a per-ticket fee. This, in effect, began training customers to pay service fees. So, when online ticket sites began to emerge, these were disruptive technologies to existing travel agencies. At Cheap Tickets, for example, there is no live agent to chat with and explore different options. There is an automated search engine that takes departure dates and times, embarkation and destination information and returns a list of possible flights and prices. There is no handling charge, either, just a nominal delivery fee. Previously, the fact that there was no handling charge would not have been an advantage, but with travel agencies routinely charging a fee, it becomes a competitive advantage.

So the online travel agency business model is very different than the brick-and-mortar model. Customers get to see, first-hand, their various travel options, and get to make their own reservations. And they can do this at three in the morning if they want to.

The number of people using online ticketing Web sites is increasing very quickly, especially those who are doing so for personal rather than for business travel. Travel agencies are still getting the bulk of business travel orders, but that is changing, too.

Longer term, it is hard to see what competitive advantage brick-and-mortar travel agencies will have over online ticket brokers. These agencies are getting squeezed by the airlines at the top, and by the online ticket brokers at the bottom. An e-business counter-strategy becomes a viable option, but not by managers used to the travel agency business model and processes. Here, clearly, the e-business model represents a disruptive technology that is already assaulting brick-and-mortar travel agencies' mainstream markets.

IS e-BUSINESS A DISRUPTIVE TECHNOLOGY FOR THE AUTOMOBILE INDUSTRY?

Now, let's look at the automobile industry. Traditionally, it was based on the horse-trading business. That is, the price of a car was based on whatever the customer was willing to pay for it. The so-called sticker price was a starting point for high-pressure sales tactics and psychological warfare. It was, again, a case of asymmetric information that favored the seller rather than the buyer. Furthermore, salespeople were pressed to sell "from inventory." Although dealers will order cars to their customers' specifications, they would rather close the deal, have the customer drive the car off the lot (thus legally taking delivery) and optimize their return on investment by stopping the ticking clock of finance interest and inventory costs.

The customer had no real idea how much a car cost the dealer, and dealers worked to keep things that way. However, consumer reports and others began to tear away at the asymmetric information fabric by publishing reasonably accurate dealer costs figures, thereby arming buyers with critical negotiating information.

Another change to the automobile business model was the buying clubs that offered auto club members, such as those who subscribe to AAA, a guaranteed fixed price for specific makes and models. In effect, selected car dealers agreed to take slightly lower profits in exchange for having buyers driven to them by the clubs. Then GM's Saturn Corporation established a policy of selling cars at the posted sticker prices and succeeded in attracting buyers who were intimidated by the usual high-pressure car-buying experience.

None of these market changes really constituted a disruptive technology. But autobytel.com's use of the Web is a different situation. Here, a single Web site offers its visitors the option of selecting specific makes and models, then gives them a "no-haggle" price and the location of the appropriate alliance dealer. In addition, it offers visitors the opportunity to finance the purchase and buy car insurance, all without leaving the comfort of their homes or offices. In turn, autobytel.com gains revenues from the car sale, the financing and the insurance sale. What's more, there's no apparent prejudice toward any make or model.

Although autobytel.com doesn't provide made-to-order services, it does allow the visitor to fully configure the selected car (color, optional features, and so on) then searches its database to find that car. The effect is one of a made-to-order purchase made possible by aggregating the inventory information of its alliance dealers. Rather than a two- to six-week wait, the customers are, ostensibly, able to get the exact car they want within a day or two.

As we said before, dealers like to sell from inventory and customers prefer to buy the specific configuration they have in mind. These two desires are not conducive to closing the sale. Thus, the ability of customers to get what they want, when they want it, and at no-hassle competitive prices is a disruptive technology for the large, traditional car manufacturers of the world.

It would be difficult for a conventional motor company to set up a one-to-one e-business where it built cars on demand and shipped them to the customer's nearest affiliated dealer. This would upset the dealer channel status quo. Clayton Christensen agrees with that assessment, too. At the same time, the buying experience through an autobytel.com will begin to compete with the traditional automobile purchase process. So far, fewer than two million customers have purchased through autobytel.com. That's a pittance in the automotive world. But remember that the mainstream market for 8-inch disk drives also turned up its nose at the prospect of 5.25-inch drives before it switched completely to the smaller form factor.

What this says about conventional automobile manufacturers is that it would be inadvisable to antagonize their dealer channels by directly developing a one-to-one e-business that could make the dealers feel disintermediated. Christensen believes a foreign automobile manufacturer, lacking a strong US dealer channel, might have an easier time establishing a first-mover presence on the Web.

IS e-BUSINESS DISRUPTIVE FOR OTHER MANUFACTURERS?

Is e-business a disruptive technology for Cisco, Intel, or any other manufacturing company that has been diligently automating all aspects of its business, and has experience with direct sales? No. It is decidedly sustaining. For these two companies, and others with similar business models and processes, the Web is an enabling factor for creating new value, increasing efficiency, lowering operating costs and increasing customer loyalty. As such, an e-business venture can, and typically should, be undertaken from within the organization.

However, there certainly are other factors involved in whether to create and manage the e-business within the parent company or as an autonomous outside company. From a market capitalization standpoint, one could argue that none of the parent company dot.com efforts have driven up the valuation as fast as independent born-on-the-Web efforts. That may be so, but it may have little relevance to the excellence of the e-business effort. We believe that, longer term, it is excellence, much more than any effect upon valuation, that should drive the decision of whether to go in-house or outside.

Keep It? Or Spin It Off?

☐ If it's disruptive — spin it off

☐ If it's sustaining and consistent with cost and culture — keep it

☐ If it's sustaining but inconsistent with cost and culture — spin it off

CHAPTER 8

Preparing for the Unpredictable

On February 7, 2000 the Yahoo! Web site was hobbled by a hacker attack. Then on February 8, 2000 Amazon.com, eBay.com, CNN.com and Buy.com were attacked in the same way. In each case, the Web sites under attack were overwhelmed by bogus requests for service and became unusable for hours at a time. Authorities are still trying to figure out whether this was the work of a group of hackers or the work of a single hacker. If the latter scenario turns out to be correct, it means that millions of potential e-commerce dollars could be lost because of the actions of a single person.

In many ways, the Web's accessibility is its Achilles heel. There are obvious reasons to make it as easy and fast as possible for online users to access Web sites, but that also makes it easier for a hacker to deploy a denial-of-service attack like the ones discussed above.

"Terrorism is a non-idle threat," says Vint Cerf. "If it were a trivial thing to destroy the power grid or Internet, we'd all be very vulnerable. Unfortunately, security can get lost in the efforts of Internet service providers to keep up with capacity demand."

Back in the 1970s, a spate of hijackings led the airline industry to push for heightened airport security. That, in turn, led to today's metal-detector protected gates. In a similar way, Web sites can be outfitted with filters that can detect the kind of hacker attacks that have occurred. But like the airline gate portals, it is the equivalent of running baggage through the x-ray system and emptying one's pockets of coins and keys. It slows things down.

These hacker attacks are examples of unpredictable events. Some Web sites will be better equipped than others to deal with such threats. That's one example of what we mean by being prepared for the unpredictable.

ANOTHER KIND OF PREPARATION

The key to preparing for the unpredictable in a larger sense is to "optimize for adaptability," says KPCB's Vinod Khosla. "In the past, IT was optimized for cost or function, but this makes far less sense in the face of a rapidly changing environment. IT's new role is to define evolvable systems. That takes a different kind of CIO," according to Khosla.

Pete Solvik, Cisco System's CIO, is Khosla's CIO role model. "He built an evolvable system," Khosla explains, "and that's why Cisco can now close their books so quickly and keep so much information available online." In fact, Khosla believes that in today's Internet Revolution, "the CIO may be more important than the vice president of marketing."

Asked for an example of an evolvable system, Khosla immediately says, "Linux." He continues, "If you look at how (Windows) NT was built and how Linux was built, Linux was built

"Terrorism is a non-idle threat. If it were a trivial thing to destroy the power grid or Internet, we'd all be very vulnerable. Unfortunately, security can get lost in the efforts of Internet service providers to keep up with capacity demand."

    – Vint Cerf
      Senior Vice President
      MCI WorldCom

to be changed and customized. It was architected as an evolvable system. It takes care of itself and is more reliable, more robust and less costly than NT."

So, one way to prepare for the unpredictable is to create a system that can evolve and scale with changes as they occur. Another way is to do what Apple did in that videotape discussed earlier in these pages. Look at what's new and extrapolate it into the future. Apple tried to extrapolate over 30 years; we'd suggest sticking with two or three at most.

STARTING WITH VISION

We thought it would be provocative to ask our cast of executive interviewees to project ahead two years and describe their Internet environment. What kinds of systems are they using to access the Net? What kinds of Net access are they using? What can they do on the Net in two years that they cannot do now?

Remember, our group of interviewees includes the CEOs of Cisco, Computer Associates, CMGI and E.piphany, plus the person who created TCP/IP and is often called the father of the Internet. We also interviewed

> "Optimize for adaptability. In the past, IT was optimized for cost or function, but this makes far less sense in the face of a rapidly changing environment. IT's new role is to define evolvable systems.
>
> —Vinod Khosla
> General Partner
> Kleiner Perkins
> Caufield & Byers

the president and COO of Priceline.com, a general partner of a VC firm that is a Silicon Valley institution, a Harvard professor who wrote a popular and respected business book and a Microsoft vice president of e-business solutions. This is an interesting mix of people with very different experiences and perspectives.

Interface Shifts to a Combination of Data, Voice and Video

John Chambers, Cisco's CEO, believes that in the future we will "access technology from a host of devices — on our bodies, in our cars, at work and at home. The basic interface will change, too, from primarily data and e-mail, to data, voice and video combined."

People-to-People, Machine-to-Machine, and Intelligent

Charles Wang, chairman and CEO of Computer Associates International, Inc., says we'll be using all kinds of different systems to access the Internet. "We'll be using things like Web TV, Palm Pilots, PCs, other handheld devices." And, says Wang, it won't all be people-to-people applications. "Your car will have Web access to help you navigate using GPS, and to perform online preventative maintenance and service."

Wang sees a lot of change at hand with better object-based databases. "Hybrids (relational databases with some object functionality) are not workable. The benefits of object-orientation are lost in the translation. That's why we [CA] went with a pure-object solution [Jasmine]." In Wang's view, pure object databases at the heart of Web operations will permit much richer and faster Web site dynamics.

Wang also expects to see more intelligence in systems. "Your point about systems that change themselves is not far-fetched." CA's Jasmine uses Neugents, software based on neural network technology as the basis for sophisticated business information analysis. They use Neugents for the automatic generation of prospect lists for new services and products, both to predict future demand for products and to enable businesses to produce just the right amount at the right time. Neugents can also determine anomalies in business, such as unusual risk and fraud. "With all the rest of the system operating at Internet speeds, a technology like Neugents may allow the e-business system to adapt to a variety of changes on the fly," Wang adds.

> **"With all the rest of the system operating at Internet speeds, a technology like Neugents may allow the e-business system to adapt to a variety of changes on the fly."**
> – Charles Wang
> Chairman and CEO
> Computer Associates
> International, Inc.

Adaptive to Me and My Interests

"I'll probably be using a PDA and a cell phone, connected by fixed, high-bandwidth, wireless access and using voice recognition to interface with the system," says David Wetherell, CMGI CEO. "There's so much you'll be able to do as bandwidth increases. You'll see rich media ads, for example. But the experience will be much more targeted and adaptive. The system will know what I'm interested in and provide it to me. If I change my interests, it will detect that and adapt."

Tetherless Connections Remove Constraints

E.piphany's CEO, Roger Siboni, thinks the next quantum leap will involve new things you can do with databases. "The real power of the Web is limited by the scalability of data and transactions, the width of the pipe [connectivity bandwidth], and that you generally have to be tethered to have a rich Web experience." Siboni sees breakthroughs in scaling, bandwidth and mobility. "I see ample bandwidth whether we're tethered or untethered. I see a time of no constraints."

More Wireless, More Machine-to-Machine Traffic

Vint Cerf, senior vice president at MCI WorldCom, and co-inventor of TCP/IP, was relieved at only having to look ahead two years. Some of his presentations deal with interplanetary networks linking the Earth with Mars, for example. "Looking at 2002, the probability is very high that I will have a radio connection at 128 Kbps — maybe bursting at 2 Mbps. Almost certainly I will be watching TV over the Net using a 400 Kbps feed. I'm already listening to radio and making phone calls this way."

Cerf also expects to be paying all his bills online and making use of Internet "bots," software agents that do things for you without your intervention. Recently, Cerf said, he was taking part in 10 simultaneous auctions on eBay by using auction "bots" to handle his bidding. "I was the winning bidder in all ten, too," he added.

But Cerf believes, in terms of sheer population of use, "The next big jump comes with Internet-enabled appliances — things around the house, in the car, things you wear, all becoming programmable." He believes that tetherless access will generate the next big Internet explosion. "There will be more traffic among these appliances than among people," he predicts. He also believes that XML is going to be a big help. "It will refine our ability to do searches, allowing us to describe materials in a more precise way. XML across industries will create an unconstrained EDI environment."

Net as Accessible as Electrical Power

Dan Schulman, Priceline.com president, sees many changes coming. "First of all, I see the Internet becoming as available as electricity. It will be everywhere around us, like electrical outlets." Schulman also envisions human interface evolution. "Voice recognition is just around the corner. You'll be able to look at that large screen and say, 'Give me the price on that stock.'" In two years time, though, Schulman sees the PC as still being the central interface mechanism with wireless handheld appliances and TV with Internet set-top boxes becoming more pervasive.

Always-On Access and Real-Time Corporations

Vinod Khosla, general partner at Kleiner Perkins Caufield & Byers, sees "dial-up virtually going away." We will, he says, be served by always-on access through wireless, cable and DSL services. Like Cerf, Khosla envisions a rapidly growing amount of machine-to-machine Web traffic. "I believe we'll also see the first startling example of a real-time corporation." Any process in a company that is not real-time "is an inefficiency," according to Khosla. "I will be shocked if, within two years, at least one company isn't reporting financial results every day."

New Experiences in Online Shopping

Clayton Christensen, Harvard professor and author, envisions an interesting change in online shopping. "When I'm shopping for clothing online, I've got a digital camera on top of my desktop computer. Some companies, such as Eddie Bauer could allow me to input height, weight, body shape, and stick my face onto the cyber body. I can try the clothes on and special algorithms will show me how they will actually fit me. When that happens, online clothing retailing will really become big."

Christensen also sees the emergence of a tiered marketplace. "Some applications won't need high bandwidth, while others will need extraordinary bandwidth." These will define the tiers. He sees wireless Net access being confined to lower-bandwidth tiers, but moving up through market tiers as broadband wireless technology will enable it to do.

Multiple Devices, Multiple Accesses, Unified Personalization

Peter Boit, Microsoft's vice president of e-business solutions, sees more than a variety of devices and access. He expects the two to be unified so that whether he's in the car, in the office, or at home, there's a continuity of data and personalization. "The point is that I will use a variety of different form-factor systems and go from dedicated line, to wireless, back to dedicated. What's important is the intelligent agent that knows me as an individual, knows what I want to see, and somehow I do something that kicks off a process and brings all that information to me. It's a combination of great software and the Internet that makes 'anytime, anywhere, any device' possible," Boit adds.

LOOKING FOR CONSENSUS

Not surprisingly there are lots of points of consensus in the future-vision of our executive interviewees. Bandwidth will increase. Wireless access will become more pervasive. We'll be using all kinds of systems to access the Net — PCs, laptops, PDAs, cell phones and TVs with set-top boxes. In addition to an increase in people-to-people traffic, the Net will see an explosion of traffic between machines.

We won't just be clicking, either. Voice synthesis and recognition technologies will play an expanded role in Internet interface. And new software technologies will adapt to our individual preferences for information and commerce, keeping our activities synchronized even as we switch between access appliances and connection technologies.

SPURRING CHANGE ON

There was fear that the Internet would run out of gas because of bandwidth limitations and constraints. It's not happening, and at the rate of new bandwidth capacity through advanced fiber networking, it won't happen. Bandwidth in the network core is ample and growing.

The bottlenecks are at the network edge. Metropolitan access networks are still optimized for circuit-switched voice traffic, even though packet-switched data traffic has become the majority message type. The problem is being attacked by IP switch technology and a preponderance of technologies aimed at enabling ISPs to offer differentiated services to business customers.

The point of this information isn't to dive down into details about transport technologies, but to help make the case that, from a wired-access perspective, bandwidth will not be a limitation for businesses or b2b companies.

Access speeds have been, and continue to be, a limitation for most consumers. Despite the broadband access inroads being made by cable operators and RBOCs with their cable-access and DSL services, most home Internet users today are still accessing the Web using dial-up connections operating at under 56 Kbps.

However, look at the roll-out pace for new cable and DSL

services. Within two years most users will be accessing the Net through broadband connections. That will enable the practical distribution of products and services that can be delivered online.

Some of our interviewees cited the constraints of being tethered as limiting the richness of online experiences. Wireless access for notebook PCs and PDAs is still relatively sparse and slow. That, too, is poised to change with the adoption of 3G (third generation) standards for wireless broadband access. It will also enable a whole new generation of handheld systems that will have fast access to the Internet. Neither speed or mobility will be the inhibitors of a rich online experience. Display size and technology, though, will limit the impact and scope of any graphical user interfaces. Just think Palm Pilot compared with 17-inch CRT or an LCD monitor.

On the other hand, size will not be a constraint for audio interface. We're already seeing handheld MP3 players, for example. And if Dan Schulman's prediction of rampant voice recognition happens soon, a handheld device with broadband wireless Internet access could become a technology enabler for all kinds of new businesses.

TIERED INTERNETS

Broadband wired and wireless access technologies will provide a foundation for a variety of Internet tiers. There will be the ones that require extraordinary bandwidth — like the

400 Kbps link that Vint Cerf will use to watch TV. And there will be those that support millions of simultaneous low-bandwidth transactions. These will be the tiers that support the e-Web or machine-to-machine traffic.

A SYNCHRONIZATION OPPORTUNITY

Microsoft's Peter Boit points out an opportunity to create end-to-end personalization, regardless of Web access instrument and access technology. It would be a combination of synchronization functionality coupled with artificial intelligence algorithms. In a possible scenario, the user accesses the Web on a desktop machine and begins bidding in an online auction that will close while he or she sits in rush-hour traffic on the way home. In the car, the user switches to a voice-recognition interface, using a wireless-access appliance that continues to give voice-synthesized accounts of current bidding.

PREPARING FOR YOUR
e-BUSINESS FUTURE

In 1997, analysts pegged the total e-commerce market for 2003 to be between $200 and $300 billion. When Cisco's John Chambers looked at these projections, he "felt they were off by a factor of five to ten," he remembers. "And they were."

Chambers still thinks the e-commerce numbers for b2b and b2c are too conservative. "I wouldn't be surprised to see them up by a factor of two or three in the near future," he says.

And what are these projections? According to the Gartner Group, b2b e-business will grow to $2.18 trillion in 2002. "The b2b explosion is imminent, fueled by a combustible mixture of investment financing, IT spending, and opportunistic euphoria that is being funneled into startups and brick and mortars' e-commerce initiatives," said Leah Knight, a Gartner Group analyst. "Collectively, they will drive short-term economic disruption but, long-term, they will drive business efficiency across industries and geographies."

> In 1997, when Cisco's John Chambers looked at the most aggressive projections of e-commerce, analysts pegged the total in 2003 at between $200 and $300 billion.
> "I felt they were off by a factor of five to ten. And they were."

For its part, the Boston Consulting Group (in a December 1999 report) pegs the b2b e-commerce market at over $2 trillion by 2003. The group believes that more than 65 percent of that total will come from six sectors: retail, motor vehicles, shipping, industrial equipment, high tech and government.

Too Conservative?

If Chambers is correct about these numbers being off by a factor of two or three, then e-commerce in 2003 could see a $4 to $6 trillion total. The Internet is the ultimate guessing game. As we said, no one really knows how many people are online even. But Chambers has the credibility of having been correct last time around and having built an e-business powerhouse. He also has the unique perspective of providing much of the e-business hardware infrastructure for nearly every e-business currently on the Net.

Therefore, when he says that two years down the road the Internet and the Web "will have changed everything," and companies that haven't made their digital transformation over the next two years "will simply get left behind," you shouldn't take that lightly.

And when he goes on to say that he believes half of 1999's Fortune 500, in terms of market capitalization, both here and globally, will not be in the Fortune 500 two years from now, it should do more than just give you pause.

ARE YOU READY?

Is your e-business strategy prepared for the possible futures we've discussed?

☐ Have you gone as far as you can go to reconstruct your supply chain?

☐ Has your latency been diminished?

☐ Are your costs being driven down?

☐ Is your customer-driven digital transformation in balance with your content, community, commerce, and collaboration (the four "C"s)?

☐ Have you factored cost and culture into your decisions about transforming your company?

☐ Is technology being employed as an enabler rather than a supporter of your digital transformation?

☐ Can your system evolve?

Whether your company is in the Fortune 500 now, or aspires to be a member of this exclusive club five years from now, digital transformation is no longer an option.

You will have to look for ways to innovate and create new value for your customers. Be prepared to eat your own lunch, too. Imitation will not help you. You've got to look at how things are being done now and then do them differently. Write your own rules and change the rules of the game for everyone.

The winning strategy is fast and flexible.
The winning system is versatile and scalable.
The winning team is totally committed.
Settle for nothing less.

Bibliography

Armstrong, Arthur and Hagel, John. *Net Gain*. Boston: Harvard Business School Press, 1997.

Christensen, Clayton. *The Innovator's Dilemma*. Boston: Harvard Business School Press, 1997.

Godin, Seth. *Permission Marketing*. New York: Simon & Schuster, 1999.

Hartman, Amir and Sifonis, John. *Net Ready*. New York: McGraw-Hill, 2000.

Peppers, Don and Rogers, Martha. *Enterprise One-To-One*. New York: Doubleday, 1997.

Slater, Robert. *Jack Welch and the GE Way*. New York: McGraw-Hill, 1999.

Index